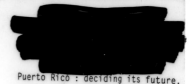

PUERTO RICO
DECIDING ITS FUTURE

PUERTO RICO
DECIDING ITS FUTURE

JUDITH HARLAN

Twenty-First Century Books
A Division of Henry Holt and Company • New York

Twenty-First Century Books
A Division of Henry Holt and Company, Inc.
115 West 18th Street
New York, NY 10011

Henry Holt® and colophon are trademarks of
Henry Holt and Company, Inc.
Publishers since 1866

Library of Congress Cataloging-in-Publication Data
Harlan, Judith.
Puerto Rico: deciding its future / Judith Harlan.—1st ed.
p.   cm.
Includes bibliographical references (p.   ) and index.
Summary: Provides a history of Puerto Rico and focuses on current concerns, such as the
possibility of statehood and the problems faced by those who come to the United States.
1. Puerto Rico—History—Juvenile literature. 2. Puerto Ricans—United States—
History—Juvenile literature. 3. Puerto Rico—Relations—United States —Juvenile
literature. 4. United States —Relations—Puerto Rico—Juvenile literature.
[1. Puerto Rico—History. 2. Puerto Ricans—United States.] I. Title
F1958.3.H37 1996
972.95dc-20   96-14714
                                                                                      CIP
                                                                                      AC

ISBN 0-8050-4372-1
First Edition—1996

DESIGNED BY KELLY SOONG

Printed in Mexico
All first editions are printed on acid-free paper. ∞
1 3 5 7 9 10 8 6 4 2

Photo credits
p. 18: Stephanie Maze/Woodfin Camp & Associates; p. 32: Bernard Boutrit/Woodfin Camp
& Associates; pp. 46, 100: Suzanne Murphy-Larronde; p. 64: Michael Massey/Gamma
Liaison; p. 74: Erich Hartmann/Magnum Photos; p. 86: Gerd Ludwig/Woodfin Camp &
Associates.

para Michelle, la poeta de la familia

ACKNOWLEDGMENTS

My first debt of gratitude goes to José Villalongo, who generously gave his time and personal insight to this project. Also, my thanks to Arnulfo Vargas at the Puerto Rican Family Institute, and to the young students who discussed the Puerto Rican question for me. My thanks to Yolanda Sánchez, executive director of the Puerto Rican Association for Community Affairs; to Maria Peralta, of the Bread and Roses Cultural Project, Inc.; to Yolanda Cabassa at the Puerto Rican Federal Affairs Administration; and to Tomás Ortiz, president of Puerto Rico in Houston, Inc.—for their insight and guidance.

CONTENTS

PUERTO RICO
DECIDING ITS FUTURE

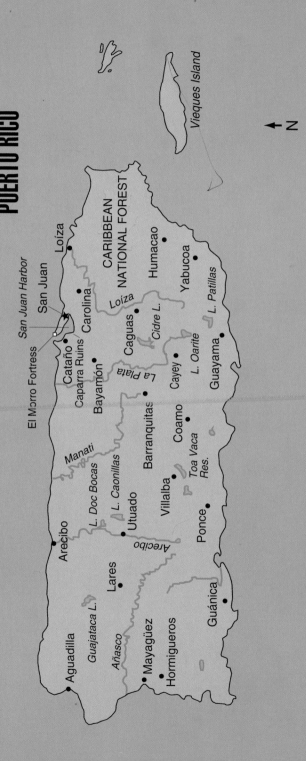

PUERTO RICO

ATLANTIC OCEAN

CARIBBEAN SEA

CARIBBEAN NATIONAL FOREST

Vieques Island

Loíza
San Juan Harbor
San Juan
El Morro Fortress
Carolina
Caparra Ruins
Cataño
Bayamón
Loíza
Caguas
Cidre L.
Humacao
Yabucoa
L. Patillas
La Plata
Cayey
L. Oarite
Guayama
Coamo
Barranquitas
Toa Vaca Res.
Villalba
Manati
L. Caonillas
L. Doc Bocas
Utuado
Ponce
Arecibo
Arecibo
Lares
Guajataca L.
Añasco
Aguadilla
Mayagüez
Hormigueros
Guánica

N

| 0 | 10 | 20 | 30 Miles |

| 0 | 10 | 20 | 30 | 40 Kilometers |

ONE

PUERTO RICAN ISSUES

. . . a culture I can identify with.

—JOSÉ VILLALONGO

"I am proud to be a Puerto Rican," writes Chris, a twelve-year-old New Yorker, "but I don't know what it means to be Puerto Rican."

Indeed. What does it mean to be Puerto Rican? That is a question that many young Puerto Ricans wrestle with, whether they live on the mainland of the United States or on the island of Puerto Rico, U.S.A.

One part of the answer is clear: Being Puerto Rican means also being American. Puerto Ricans are American citizens, and Puerto Rico is a commonwealth of the United States of America (officially called the *Estado Libre Asociado de Puerto Rico*). As a commonwealth, Puerto Rico is an associated region of the United States. So why are Puerto Ricans so often mistaken for foreigners? Is the culture and history of Puerto Rico that different from the history of the rest of the United States?

Culture and history are two of the subjects that concern leading Puerto Ricans today. Puerto Rico was ruled by Spain for four hundred years before the United States took over the island in 1898, during the Spanish-American War. Puerto Ricans have a culture, therefore, that comes chiefly from the Spanish. It combines with African and Native island cultures to form Puerto Rico's unique blend.

The culture continues to change and adapt, even today, as all cultures do, and many of Puerto Rico's latest changes are the result of the United States influence. Children learn English as well as Spanish in the island's school system. The schools are run by Puerto Rican educators, and in the classroom, teachers talk about the island's tropical bounty. They talk about its famous leaders and its Caribbean economy, but they also talk about the geography of the rest of the United States. They teach the names of American presidents, and they explain the connections between Puerto Rico and the mainland. Those connections and the flow of information back and forth between mainland and island form influences that continue to develop and change.

Puerto Ricans also watch Hollywood movies, and they read New York fashion and celebrity magazines. The influence of the current U.S. trends, personal styles, and attitudes that arrive through the media can be found throughout the island. Also, mixed in with the traditional country stores and old town plazas are discount shopping malls—places that sell the latest in American goods—and new fast-food drive-throughs.

Are all of these influences positive, though? Some Puerto Ricans see the arrival of the latest Hollywood fashions and U.S. fads as negative influences that undermine the island's traditional, Spanish culture. Others see this "modernizing" of the island as a positive thing. The limitations of the island's strict traditions are lifted for some, and these individuals are choosing to live in ways their grandparents were not allowed to. They are moving to cities and working in large corporations. They are having their own influence on Puerto Rican life.

"History made us," reads a line in one of Puerto Rico's most celebrated poems.[1] Knowing Puerto Rico's history, reports more than one Puerto Rican leader, is important for today's young Puerto Ricans. "If the youth don't know their past, they can't know and create their future," said Pilar Barbosa, Puerto Rico's official historian, in 1993.[2] And her words are echoed by other Puerto Rican leaders.

"History, understanding who we are," is necessary, says Yolanda Sánchez, the 1995 director of the Puerto Rican Association for

Community Affairs. And she adds, "If you're going to carry the tag [of Puerto Rican], then you have to have a sense of pride in what it means."[3]

That history includes many events similar to those in American history. It has its own Native Americans, European conquerors, great battles. It has great leaders and not-so-great leaders. It has its proud moments and its humbling ones. And altogether, it is a history unique to Puerto Rico, a history that defines the island and its people today. It's a history that includes the United States. It includes poetry, music, great literature, and art. It includes English, but it is mostly Spanish.

Puerto Ricans share a heritage of African, Taíno, and European ancestry. This heritage shows up in the features and skin tones of Puerto Ricans. Some are the color of cocoa, some the color of cream, some dark, some light. This heritage is a part of life on the island. For Puerto Ricans who move to the mainland, it is often a dominating theme.

DIVIDED, YET TOGETHER

Another issue of interest for Puerto Ricans is a unique one. They are a divided nation of people, with half living on the mainland of the United States. The other half of the Puerto Rican population lives on the island of Puerto Rico. Puerto Ricans, therefore, are a nation divided into two separate populations. They are divided in geography, but united in history and culture.

Puerto Ricans living on the island of Puerto Rico live in what many think of as a tropical paradise. But is it? To be certain, it has tropical breezes and beautiful, sandy beaches. But the island is overpopulated. Jobs are scarce. Money is tight.

"There are very limited opportunities on the island," says Edwin Rivera, a Puerto Rican newspaper worker in Philadelphia. He left the island and moved to Philadelphia to find work after studying at the University of Puerto Rico. He is the only one in his family who moved to the mainland, but he says he is happy he did so. Still, he adds, it is sad for him, too, when he goes home to Puerto Rico to visit. He has changed, and there is a separation now between him and them. He feels different.[4]

Puerto Ricans living on the mainland write home about the jobs and the better life they have in New York, Pennsylvania, Florida, or other states. But is that life really better? Many who moved to the mainland in the early years of migration, the 1940s and 1950s, dreamed of making enough money to go home again. Many did. Others that came to the mainland found only low-paying jobs, tenement housing, and poverty. They struggled in a different way on the mainland than they had struggled at home, but they struggled all the same.

Out of the struggles of the early Puerto Rican migrants came a community of poets, artists, and writers. They give us a picture of what it is like for the island Puerto Rican who is trying to adjust to life in the United States. They tell us, too, what it's like to be a mainland-born Puerto Rican.

A recent study of Puerto Ricans warns: Don't make the mistake of thinking that Puerto Ricans are all the same. They are not. Some are rich, some poor, some in-between. Many Puerto Ricans today have succeeded in finding good jobs and are living well.

THE QUESTION OF STATUS

Puerto Rico has two national pastimes: baseball in the winter months and the never-ending political-status debate all year, every year, says one reporter.[5] The status debate is a debate over whether or not Puerto Rico should remain a commonwealth of the United States. Its other choices are to become a state or to become an independent country. The debate has been going on for almost a century.

It is a fascinating debate because it is complicated. It involves questions about the culture of Puerto Rico. It involves questions about pride and dignity, about rights and privileges. It involves old angers and new frustrations. It is also a debate that is not going to end very soon.

Puerto Ricans living on the mainland, as well as those on the island, are caught up in the debate. Mainland Puerto Ricans, though, also are involved in state and federal politics. As of 1995, three Puerto Ricans were in the United States Congress, in addition to the commissioner from Puerto Rico. Many Puerto Ricans were state and local elected offi-

cials, too. Puerto Ricans are finding a voice in mainland p
separate from, but related to, the voice of island Puerto Ric

Puerto Ricans share a sense of culture, of what it
Puerto Rican and also American. They share this among themselves,
through their arts, literature, and community contributions, with the rest
of the American population as well.

El Morro Fortress was built by the Spaniards between
1539 and 1787 to guard the Bay of San Juan.

T W O

LAND OF THE BRAVE LORD

. . . as if they were giving their hearts.

—CHRISTOPHER COLUMBUS

Before the people came, Puerto Rico was an island of whispering seashores, wafting, warm breezes, lush, green lands, and occasionally, a wild, tree-snapping hurricane. Then the people arrived, and the island seashores still whispered and the warm breezes still wafted. And once in a while, a hurricane tore up trees and knocked down houses that the people had built across the land.

The people came from the south, up along the stepping-stones of islands that curve around the Caribbean, from the continent of South America. These islands are the Lesser Antilles. And they join the Greater Antilles (including Puerto Rico) as they stretch northward. Altogether, the region is often referred to as the West Indies.

The people came in canoes and built communities on the islands. They lived under the lush trees and celebrated their good fortune, to be living at such a good time, on such a bountiful island. Not that they didn't have to work. They did. The women tended to wide valleys of farms, growing manioc (cassava), sweet potatoes, yams, and corn. They planted the manioc in mounds, so that the tall, mature plants could serve as shelter for younger plants below them. And they planted sweet potatoes and yams in between the mounds to prevent erosion. In this way, they were able to supply much of the food their villages needed.

The men were sent out to sea to add to the food supply. They fished, captured sea turtles, and gathered mussels and oysters. They did not hunt much because there wasn't any large game on the island, but they caught rats, lizards, and birds to barbecue over a bed of charcoal. Life was good.

The people of many of these islands came to be called Taínos, and they organized their villages under *caciques* (chiefs), with one royal chief for a region, and with lesser officials ruling the villages themselves. In spiritual matters, the Taínos of Puerto Rico believed in a mother god, Guabancex[1] who lived with her male partner, Yo Cahu', on El Yunque, a rain forest where constant rain, fog-shrouded peaks, dense trees, and hills created the perfect home for the gods[2] who looked over the crops and guided the people at sea.

ARRIVAL OF THE SPANIARDS

The Taínos are the people that Columbus met when he landed on the island of San Salvador in the early-morning hours of October 12, 1492. In his journal, Columbus wrote about the generosity of the Taínos and about their gentle nature. "Of anything they have," he wrote, "they invite the person to share it, and show as much love as if they were giving their hearts."[3]

But he also wrote that the Taínos had no weapons, couldn't use them if they did, and were cowardly. So when he left a small group of his men behind when he returned to Spain, Columbus did not worry, he wrote, because "merely the people whom I have left there could destroy all that land."[4]

When he returned, in 1493, Columbus came upon some Taínos who had been captured and enslaved by neighboring hostile Indians, the Caribs. Columbus took the Taínos aboard his ship and—in trade for information about where to find gold—offered them a ride home. Their home, Borinquen (which means "Land of the Brave Lord"), is today's Puerto Rico. Columbus arrived there on November 19, 1493, and named the island San Juan Bautista.

The Borinquen Taínos wore small bits of gold, as did the Taínos of the other islands, but the immense gold mines that Columbus's men dreamed of did not exist. Most of the gold the Taínos wore had been handed down to them by their mothers and fathers. Nevertheless, the Spaniards continued to search for gold. Not surprisingly, misunderstandings arose immediately. The *caciques* of the villages met with the new forces from across the sea. They expected to offer peaceful greetings; the Spaniards met with the *caciques*, but they were expecting to take over all of the islands, and to take the islands' riches back to Spain.

The stage was set for the end of the Taínos. In the years that followed, Queen Isabella passed laws to try to protect the Taínos. But she was too far away to enforce her desires. On the islands, many Taínos were massacred or enslaved; some were even sent to Europe as slaves and sold there. Many died of overwork in the gold mines. Some committed suicide. Many others died from malnutrition because, once enslaved to work for the Spaniards, the Taínos could no longer grow their crops, and food grew scarce. Also, thousands died from the new diseases brought in from Spain—the plague, measles, smallpox, yellow fever, and influenza.

In 1511, the Borinquen Taínos rebelled. But Juan Ponce de León, the governor of the island, with experienced and well-armed soldiers, quickly overcame them. He then had six thousand Taínos put to death for the rebellion.[5]

By this time, some of the Catholic priests on the islands were trying to help the desperate Taínos. One, Fray Antonio de Montesinos, fought even harder than the others, begging the Spaniards on the islands to change their ways. During one of his church services, he asked from the pulpit: ". . . by what right or justice do you hold these Indians in such a cruel and horrible servitude? On what authority have you waged such detestable wars against these peoples, who dwelt quietly and peacefully on their own land?"[6] But the response to his questions from the Europeans on the islands was not shame or regret. It was anger. They did not want to change; they wanted to keep their slaves.

Fray Antonio de Montesinos did not give up. He went to Spain's King Ferdinand, and won the King over to his side. The King wrote the Laws of Burgos, giving some protection to the Indians. The laws took effect in 1512 and 1513.

Still, the Taínos continued to be mistreated and abused, and soon another priest, Bartolomé de las Casas, took up their cause. He wrote graphic reports of the Spaniards' massacres of the Taínos on the islands. In one, he reported on a Spanish visit to a village. The villagers gathered to greet the Spanish soldiers in peace. Then, reports de las Casas, ". . . a Spaniard . . . suddenly drew his sword. Then the whole hundred [Spaniards] drew theirs and began to rip open the bellies, to cut and kill those lambs—men, women, children, and old folk, all of whom were seated, off guard and frightened."[7]

Bartolomé de las Casas kept reporting to Spain until finally, in 1519, the Taínos were freed from slavery once and for all. But it was too late. In the few years since Columbus's arrival, the Taínos had been almost entirely killed off. In Puerto Rico, only about 4,000 Taínos were left of the estimated 40,000 to 60,000 that had lived on their tropical island when Columbus arrived.[8]

ARRIVAL OF THE AFRICANS

The Spaniards still needed workers. To replace the Taínos they had lost, they shipped in people kidnapped and enslaved from Africa.

The Africans came to a quickly changing Puerto Rico. Back in Spain, leaders saw Puerto Rico as a fortress to protect Spanish ships in the area. Military forces were assigned to the island under Ponce de León and other Spanish leaders, but Ponce de León was also beginning to see Puerto Rico as a "bread basket." He thought it would be a good place to grow food needed by the Spanish crews on their way to Peru and Mexico. Also, the gold mines were never as rich as the Spanish had dreamed, so more and more, the Europeans were turning to the agricultural riches of Puerto Rico and were establishing plantations.

Spanish hopes for the island remained high, and the island was

— EL MORRO —

In 1539, the people of Puerto Rico began building El Morro, an immense and forbidding fortress at the entrance to San Juan Bay (*el morro* means "headlands"). The fortress began with a waterfront tower of stone and mortar. Over the years, forts, tunnels, trenches, moats, and cannons were added, and El Morro rose at the sea's edge to 145 feet. By the time the building ended, three miles of walls, up to sixty feet high and sixteen feet deep on the top, had been built around much of San Juan. El Morro and some of the city's other defenses still stand today. With their great halls, towers, and dungeons, they supply a glimpse of the realities and fears of life in Puerto Rico in the first centuries of Spanish rule.[9]

renamed Puerto Rico. The legend is that when Juan Ponce de León first entered the harbor, he said, "Que puerto rico!"—What a rich port! The name stuck. Meanwhile, Ponce de León had died in Havana in 1521, from wounds he received in a fight with native tribes in Florida.

The African people on Puerto Rico were facing the same harsh conditions the Taínos had. By 1531, Puerto Rico's census listed 2,264 African slaves. They were the workforce. The Spanish population that controlled them numbered 426.[10] Africans became the farm labor, domestic servants, sugar mill workers, and labor in general. By 1540, they were almost completely out of the gold mines because the gold had been mined out.

The Africans brought their own Yoruba religion with them to the island of Puerto Rico. They also found when they arrived that many of the tropical plants and animals there were similar to those of their homeland. In short, the Africans survived, and somehow, even through the chains of slavery, they held on to some of their heritage. Through their religion and through their rituals and celebrations, their culture (chiefly a combination of West African cultures) became mixed with the Taíno and

Spanish cultures of the island, and that mixture created the beginnings of today's rich Puerto Rican culture.

ATTACKS ON THE FORTRESS

Spain was not the only country that appreciated Puerto Rico's strategic location between the Caribbean and the Atlantic. Spain's enemies in those early years also saw the value of owning Puerto Rico and they looked at the island with envy. The French, Dutch, and the English all tried to take over the island for themselves. All failed.

In one of the most famous battles in Puerto Rico's history, Sir Francis Drake, the English hero of the defeat of the Spanish Armada in 1588, tried his luck at conquering Puerto Rico. He sailed into Puerto Rican waters in 1595 with five royal ships and twenty-one other vessels. He had 4,500 men, and they expected to take the island for England. They were also after a treasure that was reported to be stored in La Fortaleza, the governor's palace.

But Puerto Rico was ready for them. Puerto Rican leaders sank two ships at the mouth of their harbor and anchored five frigates with 300 men on them behind the sunken ships. On land, more than 1,500 more Puerto Ricans and Spaniards stood guard. When the English ships were sighted at daybreak on November 22, the people of Puerto Rico were ready to fight. And fight they did, until Sir Francis Drake and his ships, suffering heavy losses, sailed away.[11]

The Dutch, then, in 1625, took their turn at trying to conquer Puerto Rico. They sailed a fleet of seventeen ships into San Juan Harbor, and they landed. They even won control of the city of San Juan. But the Puerto Rican military, holed up behind the massive walls of El Morro, would not surrender. They fought on until they began to win back their city from the Dutch. Then, in a final, desperate move, the Dutch burned the city of San Juan. The fires destroyed many homes and buildings, including the Western Hemisphere's greatest library of the time—the library of Bishop Bernardo de Balbuena. The Puerto Ricans continued to attack the Dutch until they all dived into the harbor and retreated to their ships.[12]

YEARS OF SETTLING IN

The first Spaniards to come to Puerto Rico had been adventurers, men who came with Columbus and with Juan Ponce de León. They enjoyed the adventure and the excitement of discovery, and of exploring a strange, exotic, and foreign land.

The people who followed the explorers experienced the wonder of the New World, too, but they experienced the day-to-day harshness of life there as well. They came to settle on the island. They worked in the heat of the tropical climate, through plagues, hurricanes, and attacks from hostile Carib Indians.

But still they came, and still they stayed, and life settled into a pattern. The Catholic Church played a big part in settling Puerto Rico. Catholic bishops and priests brought their religion to the Taínos, the Africans, and the Spanish colonists. They helped to establish hospitals and schools. In fact, they planted the roots of Puerto Rico's Catholic heritage.

Settlers were attracted to Puerto Rico through Spain's *encomendero* (land grant) system. Through *encomenderos*, Puerto Rican lands and slaves were granted to Spaniards who promised to work them. There was no quick and easy money—no great gold wealth—in Puerto Rico. Settlers had to work. Mostly, they farmed the land, cutting out huge plantations from the countryside. Sugar became the queen of the island. Large plantation owners became the rich elite. And the elite ran the island.

The governor of the island, though, was appointed by the Spanish monarchy, and he was the most powerful person in Puerto Rico. He controlled almost every aspect of life. He was commander of the island's military forces, had broad powers over the island's government, and even over its church. The Puerto Rican colonists themselves had no vote in any governing body.

Possibly what bothered the industrious people who settled Puerto Rico the most, though, was that Spain strictly controlled trade in and out of Puerto Rico. Commercial goods could sail only out of San Juan Harbor, and Puerto Ricans could trade only with Spain. For business-people trying to find the best market for their goods, this was a costly restriction. Not surprisingly, smuggling became a big part of the island's economy. Puerto Ricans ignored the unfair laws and shipped goods illegally to one and all. To try to gain control of the shipping in the area, Spain encouraged privateering. (Private ships were given permission to fight and capture rival ships.) The waters around Puerto Rico became almost a war zone, with Spanish, Dutch, English, and French vessels all fighting each other for the smuggled goods. Running a business in Puerto Rico became a daily challenge.

Back in Spain, the Spanish government grew more and more upset about the smuggling. Since smuggled goods were illegal, nobody was paying taxes on them. And Spain wanted those taxes!

At the same time, reports had been reaching Spain that the situation on the island was bleak. Life there was difficult when it could have been delightful. For example, wrote Fray Iñigo Abbad about that time, "The roads of this island are so rough, soggy, narrow, and dangerous that they seem more fitted for birds than for human beings."[13] Finally, in 1765, Spain sent Marshal Alejandro O'Reilly to Puerto Rico to study the island's problems. O'Reilly's report back to Spain, his *Memoria*, documented the dismal conditions.

His *Memoria* was one of the most important papers that Spain received from its colony because it prompted the monarchy to make changes. And that gave the Puerto Ricans hope. After O'Reilly's visit, a new system of land distribution began, trade laws were loosened, education was improved, and roads were built. This outpost of civilization began to become a society.

People heard that things were improving, and over the next thirty years, the population more than tripled. In 1765 Marshal O'Reilly had counted the island population at 44,883. By 1799, it was 153,232.[14] Of course, the island still had problems. In 1797, a French visitor to the island, Pierre Ledrú, wrote that "seven-tenths of the population did not know how to read due to lack of schools."[15]

But it also had new cultural achievements to brag about. Its first great painter, José Campeche (1752–1809), was creating great works of art for churches and convents. He painted the main altar of the Church of Santa Ana in San Juan. His portraits for the island's wealthy hung on the walls of their homes—homes that compared well to the lavish homes of their Spanish ancestors. Puerto Rico had its own high society, with all the fashions that go along with it—the ornate decorations in the homes, the expensive horse-drawn carriages, the parties and grand balls.

In the world around Puerto Rico, great changes were taking place, too. To the north, the American colonies were fighting for independence. In France, the citizens would soon storm the Bastille in the name of liberty. Change was in the air.

During this time, the British made one last attempt to conquer Puerto Rico. In 1797, they sent a fleet of sixty ships, carrying more than eight thousand men, into the waters off Puerto Rico. Puerto Rico's governor Don Ramón de Castro, a famed military leader, gathered his soldiers, Puerto Rico's local militia, and people and supplies from everywhere around the island.[16] The Puerto Ricans bravely fought off the attack, but the final blow was delivered by a bishop.

The bishop led a march of prayers, partly dedicated to Saint Ursula. It was night, and he and the whole town carried torches and candles through the streets as they prayed. The British mistook them for a huge oncoming army—and fled.[17]

The battle was more than just a victory for Puerto Rico. It was a coming of age of sorts. Puerto Ricans had pulled together to fight off the British, proving that Puerto Rico was no longer just a Spanish military outpost. It was a community with its own sense of identity: it was Puerto Rican.

RULE OF THE LITTLE CAESARS

Puerto Ricans soon won some reforms from Spain. They were allowed to select a local representative to send to Spain's Cortes (parliament). In 1811, they picked Navy Lieutenant D. Ramón Power y Giralt, and sent him to Spain with many requests for reforms. They wanted changes in the laws, so that, they said, "the chains that weigh us down and prevent our development be broken."[18] Under Power's leadership, Puerto Rico gained more rights: greater self-rule; immigration changes so people could immigrate to Puerto Rico from other Latin American countries; land reforms so Puerto Rican natives could get land. And they gained Spanish citizenship.

Despite the reforms, the next several years were years of hardship for Puerto Ricans. Beginning in about 1822, Puerto Rico was ruled by a series of tyrants. This was the era of the "Little Caesars." Native Puerto Ricans faced growing discrimination while the Spanish living on the island (*peninsulares*) got the best, and often the only, government positions,

---

— EL JÍBARO —

The identity of a nation is often tied up in symbols. In the United States, the symbols are of pilgrims and pioneers—women and men who came to the Americas in search of religious freedom and opportunity. In the same way, Puerto Ricans identify with the *jíbaro*.

A *jíbaro* is a poor farmer who lives a simple, honest life in the hills of Puerto Rico. He is a man who "lives in a mud hut with his family of boys and girls who are all obedient and proud of their father," explains one writer. "Each day, donning his straw hat (*una pava*), grabbing his *machete*, . . . the *jíbaro* goes off to put in fourteen hours in the fields. Here he works happily . . . , pausing only at noontime for the Angelus and a meal." The *jíbaro* is not educated, but he is not stupid. He is "shrewd," with "a natural wisdom and intelligence—something like the elder . . . of a tribe of Indians in a cowboy picture."[20]

The *jíbaro* began showing up in the first half of the 1800s, and was the title of a Puerto Rican masterpiece, *El Jíbaro*, written in 1849.[21] The *jíbaro* is not a real person, but is an ideal, a symbol. He represents the values of the Puerto Rican culture—"honesty, hospitality, warmth, and great respect for religion."[22] The *jíbaro* was one more thing that gave Puerto Ricans a sense of themselves as being separate from Spain. Today, the *jíbaro* also is a symbol that reminds Puerto Ricans of their island roots.

and everyone got better treatment than native Puerto Ricans. The governors passed rigid laws. For example, one law imposed a curfew of ten P.M. on everyone and made it illegal to have any public gathering after dark. The people grew resentful.

During this time, in 1848, the governor also passed a series of laws (*codigo negro*) that targeted African Puerto Ricans. The law ruled that anyone of African heritage who used a weapon to injure a white person would be executed. Also, slaves could be sent to prison for five years for "verbal abuse" of whites. The owners of slaves were told, too, that the government would not tell them how well to treat their slaves.[19] In effect, slave owners could be as cruel as they pleased.

Puerto Ricans had to wonder if things could get worse. Then, in 1849, things did. Governor Juan de Pezuelas passed *El Bando de Jornaleros*, a *libreta* (passbook) law. All poor adults had to carry a *libreta*. In it, the person's name, everyday behavior, debts, and work history were recorded. Any worker not carrying one was punished with eight days of forced labor. Workers also needed permission to travel between cities or even to have parties.

The *libreta* laws, of course, instead of making the people more easy to manage, made them angry. The rigid laws and the military rule of the island in general made them frustrated, too.

PUERTO RICANS FOR INDEPENDENCE

The people needed a leader to help them fight these new laws, and they found one in Ramón Emeterio Betances. In 1862, Betances gave speeches and held meetings. He told the people of Puerto Rico that it was time to stand up and fight the Spanish. For his efforts, he was sent to El Morro, and the governor threatened to hang him for treason. Legend has it that his reply to the governor was: "The night of that day I shall sleep more peacefully than Your Excellency."

Ramón Emeterio Betances (1827–1898) was a physician and a social reformer. As a physician, in 1855, he fought valiantly to overcome a cholera epidemic. It was a brutal epidemic that killed thirty thousand

Despite the rigid laws of the time and its political turmoil, this time in Puerto Rico's history, the 1800s, has often been called the golden age of cultural life.

Some of Puerto Rico's greatest poets, composers, painters, and prose writers lived and worked during this time. Lola Rodríguez de Tió wrote poetry, and so did José Gautier Benítez. Eugenio María de Hostos wrote novels, plays, children's stories, and essays. His philosophical works inspired scores of readers all over the world. Francisco Oller painted some of the great art of Puerto Rico.[23]

Life in the cities and on the large plantations could be lived with elegance, even on this remote island. Rich families built beautiful estates and had servants to keep their households clean, trim, and in running order.

people, and Betances became known for his efforts to stop it. Later, as a social reformer, Betances earned a reputation for political leadership. He led a fight to abolish slavery, and he founded the Puerto Rican Revolutionary Committee.

In 1867, Betances was thrown out of Puerto Rico for his views. While in exile, he first went to New York, then to Santo Domingo, then to Saint Thomas, and he continued his political activities. He organized a rebellion. He also issued his Ten Commandments of Freedom—a document similar to America's Bill of Rights. He demanded freedom of speech and of religion in Puerto Rico.

By today's standards, the Ten Commandments of Freedom did not make extreme demands, but the Spanish government did not want to give in to them. They wanted things to remain as they were.

Betances' followers decided to rebel. On September 23, 1868, about five hundred rebels marched into the town of Lares in western Puerto Rico. They were carrying firearms and machetes, and they captured the town. They declared it independent and founded an independent nation. They warned the Spaniards in Puerto Rico that "they had

THREE

PUERTO RICO JOINS THE UNITED STATES

*The island accepted the American invasion with great
rejoicing, which I consider premature . . .*

—LUIS MUÑOZ RIVERA

Puerto Ricans watched as the Spanish-American War of 1898 gained momentum. The war began as political friction between the United States and Spain over Spain's treatment of Cuba, one of its colonies. Newspapers reported stories of concentration camps and torture on the island, and headlines screamed for action. American businesses in Cuba sent their leaders to Washington with pleas for help. Then, while the politicians were arguing, the reporters were shouting, business leaders were pleading, and the United States was negotiating with Spain, the U.S.S. *Maine* exploded in Havana Harbor on February 15, 1898, and 260 crew members died.

Some say the explosion was from an explosive mine device; others say the explosion came from aboard the ship. Regardless, the tragedy fueled the fires of anger. Spain and the United States declared war on each other. Then the United States launched an attack on the Philippines, a Spanish colony. And it also invaded Cuba.

Finally, early in the morning of July 25, 1898, the U.S.S. *Gloucester* sailed into the quiet bay of Guánica on the southwest shores of Puerto Rico. Troops landed and planted the United States flag. Prepared for battle, they marched into the nearby town of Ponce, but there were no guns to meet them. They were welcomed with a band, a parade, and, said news reporters of the time, they were "bombarded with cigars and bananas."[1]

"We have not come to make war upon the people of a country that for centuries has been oppressed," General Nelson Miles, commander-in-chief of the American invasion, told the Puerto Ricans, "but, on the contrary, [we come] to bring you protection . . . to promote your prosperity, and to bestow upon you the immunities and blessings of . . . our government."[2]

Puerto Ricans believed and hoped that the United States, a country based on democracy, would treat them with *dignidad* and *respeto* (consideration and respect). These were two deeply cherished values in the Puerto Rican culture. Puerto Ricans saw the end of four hundred years of Spanish rule and the beginning of a new life for their island. They saw autonomy. They saw freedom close at hand. Many admired the democratic values and the government of the United States and looked to it as a model of freedom. They had high expectations.

Yet there was some hesitation among the island's leaders. Puerto

---

— THREE LEADERS OF THE DAY —

José Celso Barbosa (1857–1921) was a physician and editor. He was in favor of Puerto Rico becoming a state of the United States. He founded the Statehood Republican Party in 1899.

José de Diego (1866–1918) was a brilliant speaker and poet. He was also a statesman. "We have to learn to say 'no,' raise our lips, unburden our chest, put in tension all our vocal muscles and all our willpower to fire this o of no . . . ," he said.[3] He is remembered as a defender of independence.

Luis Muñoz Rivera (1859–1916) worked to get Spain to make changes, and then did the same with the United States.

Ricans had fought hard to gain a measure of independence from Spain, and now they had no real guarantees. Where did they stand with the new power on the island, the Americans? They did not know for sure.

Luis Muñoz Rivera expressed his concern. He advised Puerto Ricans to hold "a noble and sober reserve until the thinking and action of the Washington legislature" was revealed.[4]

MILITARY RULE OVER THE ISLAND

Were Muñoz's instincts right? Certainly, the first few years of American rule were steps backward for the Puerto Rican people. The island was put under strict military rule. Some historians refer to these first two years as the rule of the American "Czars and Sultans" because the generals had tremendous power over the affairs of the island. Often they used that power without asking the Puerto Ricans for their opinions.

Under military rule, Muñoz Rivera was dismissed from his governorship in 1899; the press was censored; and new laws were made on education, the courts, and the cities. Many Puerto Ricans, as they watched these unasked-for changes take place, became disheartened. They saw that they had even fewer liberties than they had had under Spanish rule.

José Henna, a Puerto Rican who had supported the United States takeover, expressed the views of many of his fellow Puerto Ricans when he said in 1900, ". . . the [American] occupation has been a perfect failure. We have suffered everything. No liberty, no rights, absolutely no protection, not even the right to travel. We cannot travel today because we cannot get passports. We are Mr. Nobody from Nowhere. We have no political status, no civil rights. That cannot go on very long."[5]

Life on the island was thrown into temporary chaos. Because Puerto Rico was no longer part of Spain, Puerto Ricans had to pay high tariffs to sell their sugar in Europe. Tariffs are taxes that governments place on imports and exports. With tariffs, governments control the price of incoming goods, so that their own goods cannot be undersold. Tariffs on exports tax outgoing goods.

The new tariffs that Puerto Ricans had to pay meant that their sugar was more expensive in Europe and people there simply wouldn't buy it. Meanwhile, in the United States market, Puerto Ricans faced long-standing tariffs on their sugar, tariffs that the United States government had not yet lifted. Also, tobacco and coffee markets were suffering. And, to make matters worse, the exchange of the Spanish peso for the United States dollar, Puerto Rico's new currency, was set so that Puerto Ricans lost money on each exchange. Once again, it seemed that things could not get worse.

Then Hurricane San Ciriaco hit on August 8, 1899. More than three thousand people died; the coffee crop was destroyed; plantain trees were uprooted and washed away. The island was a disaster zone. So what was the average islander thinking? The people had just seen their country given from Spain to the United States, their leaders deposed, their economy changed from the peso to the dollar, a drop in the market for their crops, and a hurricane. Some, no doubt, wished for a return to the old days. Others were still hopeful about the future. All watched the new occupying forces closely and with growing suspicion.

Puerto Rican leaders wanted something done, and done quickly, to get rid of the U.S. military rule over their island. They thought that they might have a friend in President McKinley. The president said he wanted Puerto Rico to have "the best possible form of government."[6]

But from the beginning, it was apparent that United States leaders and politicians defined that form of government differently than Puerto Ricans defined it. The same leaders also saw the Puerto Rican people differently than they saw themselves. Americans did not value Puerto Rico's four hundred years of Spanish civilization. Americans also did not see the sophistication of the island leaders, who had fought many long battles through many long years to gain some power in Spain over their own affairs.

Americans did not see the depth or the maturity of the culture of Puerto Rico, but noticed instead that the island population of about 950,000 people was mostly a rural society. They saw that farming was the major occupation on the island[7] and that 80 percent of the population could not read or write.[8] They saw that overall, living standards on the island were lower than in the United States.

Also, Americans thought of Puerto Ricans as different, and at that time in U.S. history "different" usually meant "not as good." The attitude toward the island very quickly became paternalistic (fatherly)—in much the same way as Europe's attitude was toward its colonies. The United States would be the parent to the child Puerto Rico. Puerto Rico would learn how to think, act, and do things the American way. Not all Puerto Ricans were pleased at being treated like children. In fact, many were insulted.

DISAPPOINTMENT IN NEW RULERS

At last, in 1900, President McKinley signed the Foraker Act, and military rule ended. Puerto Rico was named a territory, and its new American form of government officially began.

Under the act, Puerto Ricans would elect thirty-five members to their own Puerto Rican House of Delegates (similar to the U.S. House of Representatives) to make laws on island affairs. But the United States would also appoint an eleven-member council (similar to the U.S. Senate), only five of whom were Puerto Rican. Also, the United States president would appoint a governor of Puerto Rico who would have final say over these affairs. In addition, the U.S. Congress in Washington, D.C., had absolute power to annul any law passed in Puerto Rico. Puerto Ricans were allowed to elect a commissioner to represent their interests in the U.S. Congress, but the commissioner would not be allowed to vote in Congress.

Puerto Rican leaders were disappointed. They still had less power over their island affairs than under Spanish rule. And, to make matters more difficult, the United States imposed a tariff on Puerto Rican sugar and tobacco going to U.S. markets. This was to protect the U.S. industries from Puerto Rican competition.

Political leaders on the mainland as well as on the island stood up to criticize the Foraker Act. The act is "unworthy of the United States which imposes it and Puerto Ricans who have to endure it," asserted Luis Muñoz Rivera. The Democratic Party stood by Muñoz Rivera, and in an official statement, called the act "a flagrant breach of national good faith."[9] In brief, they said, it was stingy.

CHANGES ON THE ISLAND

But, disappointed or not, Puerto Ricans found that life went on. Many things remained the same. Children asked for *granizados* (tropical fruit ices), and parents bought them when they could. For dinner, *habichuelas con arroz* (beans and rice) remained a favorite for Puerto Rican families. The Caribbean breezes still wafted over the tops of their trees, and *plataños* (plantains) still tasted delicious when sliced up and fried.

Changes came, too. Protestant ministers arrived to assert their influence over the chiefly Catholic population. And the United States immediately set to work improving medical and sanitation facilities in Puerto Rico. People were vaccinated against smallpox, and parents had modern doctors to attend to their children. Within ten years, the death rate in Puerto Rico fell to 22 per 1,000, which was better than the rates in surrounding countries.[10]

As soon as the United States took over Puerto Rico, Spanish, the language of Puerto Rico, came in conflict with English, the language of Puerto Rico's new, U.S. government. The conflict over English and Spanish, though, was not really over language. It was over a larger cultural and political conflict. Everyone agreed that it was a good idea to learn English, but if that meant losing Spanish, then that would be "Americanization." Puerto Ricans already had a Spanish culture. They did not want to lose it and they feared that they might because language is an important part of culture.

Nevertheless, children were put into United States–style classrooms. At first, the U.S. government tried to teach all classes in English. That didn't work. So over the next fifty years other systems were tried. During some of those years, elementary classes were taught in Spanish and high school in English. In other years, classes were taught in Spanish, and English was a subject during the lower grades; then in high school, classes were taught in English and Spanish was a subject. The goal in all of the programs was for all students to be fluent in English by the end of high school. Some of the programs also sought the goal of full bilingualism.

Schools were built quickly. In 1901–1902, there were 874 public schools in Puerto Rico, with 42,070 pupils; in 1909, there were 1,912 public schools, and 114,367 pupils.[11] In 1903, the University of Puerto Rico was founded. Clearly, education was a priority in an American-run Puerto Rico.

U.S. CITIZENSHIP FOR ALL

Puerto Ricans were still not citizens of the United States, though, and that fact continued to be an issue until 1917. In that year, the U.S. Congress passed the Jones Act and President Woodrow Wilson signed it. The act granted citizenship to every Puerto Rican who wanted it.

Also, more political power was passed into the hands of Puerto Ricans. The Puerto Rico council was no longer appointed by the president. It was elected by the people of Puerto Rico, and so it was truly a Puerto Rican Senate. However, the governor was still appointed by the president and still had powers over the budget. The governor also had veto power over the Puerto Rican House and Senate, but now the island's House and Senate could overrule the governor with a two-thirds vote. Puerto Rican legislation still went to Washington for approval by the president. All of these changes were welcome because they meant that Puerto Ricans had more power over their affairs. But the U.S. federal government was still a very strict supervisor of Puerto Rican affairs.

The world around Puerto Rico was in chaos. World War I began and the United States entered the war in 1917. Puerto Ricans were United States citizens, and they fought in the war just as mainland citizens did. During the war, eighteen thousand Puerto Ricans served in the U.S. military. Also, Puerto Rican people donated thousands of dollars to the war effort, and they bought more than $10 million in war bonds. It had been two decades since the beginning of Puerto Rico's close ties with the United States, and Puerto Ricans had begun to become a part of the great monolith from the north.

DISCONTENT ON THE ISLAND

Conflict over the politics, economics, and education of the people continued. Puerto Ricans were searching for answers and for new ways of

— PEDRO ALBIZU CAMPOS —

Pedro Albizu Campos (1893–1965) was born in Ponce, Puerto Rico. While a student at Harvard, he became deeply impressed with the Irish fight against British rule. He thought the fight was very much like the fight in his own homeland, Puerto Rico.

When he returned to Puerto Rico, Albizu Campos tried to work for change from within the system. He ran for office in 1932, calling for complete independence for Puerto Rico. Thousands of people came to listen to his "sharp, staccato phrases . . . his clear, merciless logic."[12] But he received very few votes (just over 11,000 out of 382,722). After the election, he lost all faith in the system and grew more and more militant. He led his followers in violent conflicts with the Puerto Rican and U.S. governments. As a result of some of these fights, Albizu Campos was jailed three times, spending a total of almost two decades of his life in federal prisons.

relating to the world now that they were no longer a Spanish possession. Some called for closer relations to the United States. Others wanted things to continue as they were. In the 1920s, a voice for complete independence began to be heard—the voice of Pedro Albizu Campos.

In 1930, Pedro Albizu Campos was in Puerto Rico delivering speeches on nationalism (independence). He began each of his political meetings by singing the Puerto Rican national anthem, and he had a flag, a one-star banner. The anthem and the flag gave the people a symbol, and the symbol worked as patriotic symbols are meant to work. It added to the depth of their feelings, so that they could become united emotionally as well as politically. During the 1932 campaigns, some of this patriotic fervor turned to violence, and Albizu Campos was in the background as the violence and riots broke out.

In 1937, a group of Albizu Campos's Nationalists held a march in the streets of Ponce. The police moved in to stop them. The marchers fought back, and by the end of the fight, nineteen people were dead and more than one hundred wounded. The day became known as the day of the Ponce Massacre, and is still remembered today as a symbol of Puerto Rico's struggle for independence.

Feelings for independence ran deep with many people on the island during that time. One famous Puerto Rican poet who fought for independence was Julia de Burgos. She called her fellow Puerto Ricans "my enslaved people." And she wrote of the Río Grande de Loíza, a great river in Puerto Rico. She called the Loíza a river of tears that flowed because it was sad that Puerto Ricans were enslaved.

While Albizu Campos was fighting for independence, another Puerto Rican leader was gaining importance—Luis Muñoz Marín. He founded a new political party in 1938, the PPD (Partido Popular Democrático). On the party's flag was a picture of a *jíbaro*, and the party's motto was *Pan, Tierra, y Libertad* (bread, land, and liberty).

The party began as a party seeking independence, but through nonviolent methods. (Later, this party changed to support staying with the United States.)[14]

The 1930s were a time of hardship throughout much of the Western world. The Great Depression, which was signaled by the stock market crash of 1929, was on. All over the world people struggled just to find food and shelter for themselves and their children. Meanwhile, Puerto Rico was still trying to recover from a devastating hurricane that had swept across the island in 1928. Hurricane San Felipe had brought

---

— **THE SONG OF PUERTO RICO** —

A poet, Lola Rodríguez de Tió, in 1868, wrote the lyrics of the revolutionary anthem, "La Borinqueña," and it became a cry for liberty during El Grito de Lares in 1868. Since her version, several changes have been made. But today, "La Borinqueña" is still sung as the hymn of Puerto Rico. Its most well-known version celebrates the beauty, charm, sun, and sea of Puerto Rico. "The sky is ever clear," says the song, and the land is surrounded by softly cresting surf.[13]

winds of over 160 mph and thirty inches of rain in two days to the central mountain region. The hurricane had destroyed an estimated fifty thousand homes. It ruined crops, sugar mills, tobacco factories, warehouses, and fruit packing plants, and put thousands of people out of work.[15]

With the double blow of Hurricane San Felipe and the depression, Puerto Rico's island economy suffered desperately. Many people in Puerto Rico in 1934—42 percent according to one analyst—were receiving welfare relief from the United States federal government.[16]

As Puerto Ricans struggled with the question of their own government and their own economy, the world around them once again was heading for war, World War II. In this war, 65,000 Puerto Ricans served in the U.S. military.

The United States looked at Puerto Rico with renewed interest, too, because Puerto Rico was a good place for military bases. Once again, as it had been in the first centuries of its life, Puerto Rico was a "strategic location," and American military bases were established there.

A COMMONWEALTH AT LAST

The war proved once again that Puerto Ricans had become an important part of the United States. And things were about to change dramatically for the islanders. Puerto Rico had been in American hands for forty-eight years when in 1946 President Truman appointed the first Puerto Rican, Jesús Piñero, to be governor of the island.

The following year, 1947, the United States Congress passed the Elective Governors Act. The president would no longer appoint a governor for Puerto Ricans. They would now elect their own, and that governor would appoint most of the officials on the island. This meant that the Puerto Ricans themselves would have almost full control over their own affairs.

This decision did not come about on its own. It was the hard-won result of years of political discussion and wrangling. One of the leaders of the Puerto Rican struggle for the right to more self-government was

42

Luis Muñoz Marín. Muñoz Marín became the first elected Puerto Rican governor.

One of Muñoz Marín's first acts as governor was to appoint an educator, Mariano Villaronga, as commissioner of education. Villaronga held the view that schools in Puerto Rico should be taught in Spanish, with English as a second language. "This was an important gain in self-government in a very sensitive area, involving cultural values and feelings," explains Arturo Morales Carrión, a Puerto Rican political historian.[17] Language and culture are interwoven, so that a renewed respect for the Spanish language in Puerto Rico meant also a renewed respect for the Spanish heritage of the island.

Muñoz Marín believed that the best option for Puerto Rico was a relationship of mutual consent with the United States. He sought local self-government in association with the United States. He wanted Puerto Ricans to keep their American citizenship and common market with the United States, but to have complete power over their own affairs. Muñoz

---

— LUIS MUÑOZ MARÍN —

Luis Muñoz Marín (1898–1980) was the son of Puerto Rico's leader, Luis Muñoz Rivera. He was born just a few days before the Spanish-American War began, and because of his father's position, he learned about the politics of Puerto Rico as he grew up.

Muñoz Marín became a gifted poet, a journalist, and an intellectual spokesperson for Puerto Ricans. "A good civilization," he wrote in a 1960 speech to the Puerto Rican Legislative Assembly, "it seems to me, is one which continues to work energetically to create more wealth, but directs this wealth toward the fulfillment of deeper values."[18]

Muñoz Marín hoped that Puerto Rico could be a separate, but associated, region of the United States. He was part of the Puerto Rican body that worked on Puerto Rico's Constitution, which was adopted in 1952.

Marín was successful at convincing not just the people in Puerto Rico but also the people in the U.S. Congress that he was right.

In 1950, the United States Congress passed Public Law 600. This law allowed Puerto Ricans to vote to become a commonwealth of the United States and to write their own Constitution, one that would work alongside the Constitution of the United States. This was one of the greatest changes yet for Puerto Rico. It was not without controversy, however. Nationalists, under the leadership of Albizu Campos, fought against further development of ties with the United States.

Nationalists expressed their views with acts of terrorism. They attacked Governor Muñoz Marín's governor's palace and were fought off by a handful of the governor's defenders. Five Nationalists were killed and two police officers wounded that day. Nationalists also attacked Blair House in Washington, D.C., where President Truman was living while the White House was being repaired. They, too, were repulsed. The terrorism did not change the minds of Puerto Ricans who voted for a Constitutional Convention, with 387,016 votes in favor and 119,169 against.[19]

On July 25, 1952, Puerto Rico's new Constitution took effect. Muñoz Marín proudly raised the Puerto Rican flag above El Morro. The flag, the official emblem of the Estado Libre Asociado de Puerto Rico (free associated state, or commonwealth), was originally created by Puerto Ricans in 1895.

Puerto Rico now elects its own governor and legislature, and appoints its own judges, all cabinet officials, and all other lesser officials, in the executive branch. It sets its own educational policies, determines its own budget, and amends its own civil and criminal code. It now has greater power over its own destiny than it ever did before.

AMERICANIZATION OF PUERTO RICO

The political health of a country works hand in hand with its economic health. And the economy of Puerto Rico was another problem that Muñoz Marín tackled. He became one of the moving forces behind Operation Bootstrap. This was a plan for developing business on the island. Part of it was a tax law that allowed businesses generous tax breaks for opening plants in Puerto Rico. Organizers hoped that the island could attract business, which would bring jobs.

Puerto Rico offered low taxes to businesses because Puerto Ricans do not pay federal taxes. It also offered cheap labor, compared to the United States, and it had access to the U.S. market. Because of Operation Bootstrap, the 1950s were promising years for the island's economy. When Muñoz Marín addressed the legislature in 1960, he was able to talk about new factories operating on the island, increased farm production, and pay raises for Puerto Rican workers.

It might seem that Puerto Rico had turned into a paradise for one and all—but not so. In 1954, four Puerto Rican Nationalists, dramatizing their desire for independence, opened fire on the U.S. House of Representatives, wounding five congressmen. Albizu Campos called this act of terrorism "sublime heroism."[20]

But Puerto Rico's ties with the United States were well established by this time. In fact, many Puerto Ricans were complaining of becoming too "Americanized." Hotels were attracting American tourists. American movies and television shows were becoming part of island life. Material goods—cars, trendy clothes, kitchen appliances, and disposable goods—quickly found their way into Puerto Rican life. Puerto Ricans wanted these products, but the products also became symbols for the things that people don't like about American society.

Some things about America, however, were accepted as positive factors. Baseball was one of these. Puerto Rican baseball player Roberto Clemente (1934–1972) became one of Puerto Rico's most celebrated heroes. He joined the Pittsburgh Pirates and became famous as their all-star right fielder. In his eighteen-year baseball career, between 1955 and 1972, he had three thousand hits and a .317 career batting average.

He was most loved, though, not for his baseball but for his generosity. Throughout his life he reached out to give personal help to people in need. He died in 1972 while flying supplies to victims of an earthquake in Nicaragua. "He was always giving to people, especially the people of Puerto Rico, the blue-collar people who get overlooked. His pockets were open. His house was open," one admirer said.[21] That generosity, that willingness to share—is what being Puerto Rican is all about.

Education is of primary importance in Puerto Rico.
About ninety percent of the population can read and write.

FOUR

LIFE ON THE ISLAND TODAY

. . . a very complicated life, full of challenge.

—JUAN GONZALEZ

When people in San Juan talk about traveling, they say they will travel "to the island"—*en la isla*. When they return, they say they come back from the island. In places *la isla* is a tropical paradise with long, sweeping beaches of pale sand and warm, calm waters with coconut palm trees lining the beaches. In other places, *la isla* is a desert with cacti and dry skies. In yet others it is a rain forest or a ranch or a sugarcane field or a farm.

People like to call the island a tropical paradise because it almost always feels like summer in Puerto Rico. The average temperature all year round ranges from seventy to eighty degrees. It rains on the island in wonderful amounts, ranging from an average of twenty inches on the southwestern coast to sixty inches on the northeastern coast. At the high elevations of the Caribbean National Forest, it rains more than two hundred inches in a year.[1] The island is green and lush and full of the promise of blue skies and tropical fruit.

The beauty of the island has inspired poets and romantics for as long as anyone can remember. One poet, Luis Palés Matos, calls it "my green Antille."[2] Another poet, Juan Rodríguez Calderón, calls Puerto Rico "eternal spring."[3] The beauty of the island, in fact, is a theme of Puerto Rico's national anthem. It's the sentiment that fills the voices of many Puerto Ricans when they talk of their homeland.

But this tropical paradise is not all beauty. The hurricanes that whip across Puerto Rico periodically rip up the tropical serenity of the island by the roots and tear it to shreds. In 1989 Hurricane Hugo left several towns on the east coast virtually destroyed. Losses were staggering. The Red Cross reported fifty thousand people homeless, twelve thousand houses completely destroyed, and twenty thousand homes damaged. Agricultural losses were $150 million. One poultry rancher looked out over a field where ten thousand hens lay dead after the storm.

The hurricane itself was a terrifying experience for Puerto Ricans. Telephone poles were snapped in two, and hundreds of boats sank in the harbors. Whole hillsides were wiped clean of trees and plant life. Entire neighborhoods were reduced to sticks and shattered pieces of wood. Days later, reported one observer, children huddled, "trembling, close to the few walls that are left standing." They were still shaken up from spending fifteen hours under beds while their houses were blown apart above them.[4]

Another contrast to the island's rich beauty is its jarring poverty. In terms of resources, Puerto Rico is dirt poor. The gold that Columbus's men sought is long gone. The fertile farmlands that supported the Taíno people in the centuries before Columbus are still fertile, but the Taínos numbered only between forty and sixty thousand. Puerto Ricans today number 3.7 million. The overpopulation of the island is not unusual. The planet as a whole is facing a future crisis in overpopulation. But in Puerto Rico, the problem is here, today. Puerto Rico is one of the most densely populated regions on earth.

TRADITIONS AND THE OLD WAYS

Respect is an important part of the Puerto Rican culture. "You respect others because they are human and have dignity," explains Frank Solano, a Puerto Rican psychologist living in New York. A whole system of traditions builds upon this idea. Children and grown adults, too, treat their elders with respect. In Spanish, there are the words *doña* and *don*. These are terms of respect, as in Doña María or in Don Pedro. They are used with first names in familiar relationships. They add a respectful tone to what otherwise would be simply "hi, María," or "hello, Pedro." (The words *señora*, *señorita*, and *señor* are used with last names, for formal, less intimate relations.) There is no translation for *doña* and *don* into English.[5]

In Puerto Rico, also part of the culture is cooperation and sharing instead of competition, adds Edwin Rivera, who grew up in Carolina, Puerto Rico. "In America," he says, the cliché is that "nice guys finish last." In Puerto Rico, "good guys finish first." People share in Puerto Rico, he asserts, especially those who are poor. "In a poor culture, people share. They share love, caring and non-material things," he explains.[6]

The extended family, too, is another thing that Puerto Ricans talk about when they speak of Puerto Rico. Uncles and aunts and cousins and godmothers and godfathers and grandparents all pitch in to help raise the children in a family. So families are large, and rich in personalities and experiences.

Puerto Rico's population shares an exciting heritage, too, and a unique racial diversity lends its tones to Puerto Rican life. Race is not the same issue in Puerto Rico as it is in mainland America. Color is noticed, but African and Spanish and Taíno heritage is shared by much of the Puerto Rican population. "Puerto Rico has a problem of color," says Samuel Betances, a Puerto Rican who has studied the issue. But, he adds, "America has a problem of race." And there is a difference.

"Discrimination in Puerto Rico is based on color," Betances continues.[7] In general, lighter-skinned Puerto Ricans find it easier to get jobs, while darker-skinned Puerto Ricans face discrimination on their island. A phrase often used on the island, *adelantar la raza*, illustrates Puerto Rico's discrimination. *Adelantar la raza* translates into "to improve the race." What it really means, though, to the people who say it, is to make the race lighter. Young Puerto Ricans are often encouraged to marry people lighter than they are, and they are discouraged from marrying people darker than they are.[8]

Some of Puerto Rico's most famous poets and writers, however, have disagreed with *adelantar la raza* and have, instead, celebrated the island's African ancestry. In one of his poems, Matos talks about the influence of Puerto Rico's African heritage on the island's music and dance. He uses this influence on music as just one example of the many beautiful elements of Puerto Rico's African heritage.[9] Poet Rosario Morales writes, simply, that "Africa waters the roots of my tree."[10]

ROLES FOR WOMEN AND MEN

Women in Puerto Rico also face discrimination. The old rules, based on strict religious grounds, held that women were protected by fathers until marriage. Then they were under the rule of their husbands. They were expected to be virgins while single, but at the same time they were supposed to be sexually enticing. Men were supposed to be *macho*. They were not expected to be virgins while single. Even once married, if they were not faithful, society looked the other way.

The way men and women related to each other affected all of society. It affected whose voice was listened to, who was allowed to vote, who ran the government, who owned the businesses, what was taught in school, and even what games boys and girls were allowed to play.

Of course, this system of *machismo* was very limiting for women. But it was also limiting to men. Under such a system, men had just a few roles that they could play in life, and they were ridiculed if they tried to do things differently.

Today many men in Puerto Rico still suffer under the limitations of *machismo*. So do women. One woman who left Puerto Rico in 1944 talks about why she left. She says she felt "a desperate desire to break out." She was just nineteen years old, and her family did not want her to leave, but she left anyway. The woman is Antonia Pantoja, and she explains that she went to New York to find freedom and opportunity. Today Pantoja is honored as one of the founders of the Puerto Rican Forum and the organizer of ASPIRA, a national organization that helps Latino students develop leadership skills.

Another woman, Gigi Fernández, found a different way to "break out." Fernández grew up in San Juan and became a professional tennis player. She won the women's doubles title at Wimbledon in 1992, and she won at the French Open in 1991 and 1992. This would not be terribly surprising for a woman from the mainland United States, but it was highly unusual for an island Puerto Rican. In fact, she was the first female Puerto Rican athlete from the island to turn professional. "In a way it's kind of neat," Fernández told a magazine reporter, "because it's opening a door for female athletes in Puerto Rico. Before, it was taboo for a female to make a living out of a sport. Girls were supposed to get married and have kids, so now maybe this opens the door."[11]

HEROES OF THE PEOPLE

"Puerto Rico's greatest natural resource is its own people, a people who are among the most decent, intelligent, and admirable on earth," says Ronald Fernandez, a political analyst and author.[12] People are what determine the successes and failures of a country. And the people of

Puerto Rico today are upholding their tradition of placing high value on generosity. Juan Gonzalez, a major-league baseball player, explains why he thinks it is important to give time and money to his fellow islanders.

"We live a very complicated life, full of challenges," he says, so he tries to be a good example to young people. Gonzalez is from Vega Baja, a small, poor town in northern Puerto Rico. He grew up to become a baseball hero, an outfielder for the Texas Rangers and major-league home-run champion. Today, the part of town he grew up in is the site of drugs, prostitution, and poverty. "It makes me feel bad and sad at the same time," Gonzalez says of the neighborhood. "The youth is losing its future to drugs."

During his baseball career, Gonzalez returns to Puerto Rico every off-season, and he is a hero there. Like Roberto Clemente, he is idolized not just for his baseball exploits but for his generous nature as well. He helps individuals, giving vitamins to the boys who work out with him and often paying utility bills for people in need.[13]

Many Puerto Ricans talk about being role models for young people and for other Puerto Ricans in general. Living an honest and successful life, then, is something Puerto Ricans see themselves doing for others, as well as for themselves.

THE IMPORTANCE OF SCHOOLS

The Puerto Rican schools were what started Nydia Velázquez (a U.S. congresswoman) in politics. It was the late 1960s, and the Puerto Rican schools were poorly financed. Velázquez was going to high school in Yabucoa, a poor, rural area in Puerto Rico. She gathered up her fellow students and led them in a protest against dangerous and unsanitary conditions at the school, and she was successful. The school closed down until repairs were made. Education was the beginning of a successful career for Velázquez. And education in Puerto Rico today is a priority for the Puerto Rican government.

Puerto Rico devotes almost one-third of its budget to education.[14] What's more, the school system in Puerto Rico employs more people than any other part of the government. The concentration on education seems to be paying off. By the 1990s, about 90 percent of the population could read and write.

The Puerto Rican government reports that the island has six public and thirty-three private institutions of higher learning. More than 160,000 students were enrolled in these universities and colleges in the first half of the 1990s. The University of Puerto Rico reported 53,000 students, with campuses in Rio Piedras, Mayagüez, San Juan, Cayey, and Humacao. Students at the University of Puerto Rico could earn bachelor's, master's, and doctoral degrees.

Classes in Puerto Rico are taught in Spanish, as they have been since 1949, when Puerto Ricans began appointing their own commissioner of education. English is taught as a second language. Language has been an issue that is closely tied to politics, so the use of English in the classroom has varied along with political leaders. Promoters of independence have been against allowing classes to be taught in English. Promoters of statehood want students to be fluent in English.

Today, English is widely understood by the people in Puerto Rico, though only a minority speak it fluently. And the government has declared both languages official languages of Puerto Rico. The decision of whether to use Spanish or English, however, is a subject that raises emotions on the island as much as it does on the mainland. Puerto Rican poet Evaristo Ribera Chevremont refers to language as the "voice of the centuries," and he fights to preserve Puerto Rico's Spanish because he believes it represents a valuable part of the island's culture.[15]

FESTIVALS AROUND THE ISLAND

Many towns dot the island both on the coast and inland. Most have their own separate identities—sometimes farming is a focus of interest for a town, sometimes a factory, sometimes tourism. The towns all have their own festivals and unique stories.

Many of the island's festivals reflect Puerto Rico's religious heritage. About 80 percent of Puerto Ricans are Roman Catholic, and close to 99 percent are Christian. Each town has a patron saint, and every year, the town holds a celebration in honor of its saint. Usually, a town has a carnival with a Ferris wheel, games of chance, music, dancing, and food.

In San Juan, a unique tradition is added as part of the celebration of its patron saint, John the Baptist. On that day, at midnight, *sanjuaneros* traditionally walk into the sea backward three times for good luck through the coming year. San Juan shows its more sophisticated side, though, when it hosts the Festival Casals, an international music festival founded by cellist Pablo Casals.

In the town of Hormigueros on the west coast of Puerto Rico, a very solemn holiday is celebrated every year: the feast day of Our Lady of the Monsarrat. During this day, the devout climb the steep stone steps to the church on their knees. Another solemn Christian holiday that is celebrated throughout the island is Good Friday. This is the day that commemorates the day Jesus Christ died on the cross. On Good Friday, Puerto Rico is the scene of numerous somber parades, Catholic masses, and other church services.

A few Puerto Rican festivals focus on a combination of the African and Spanish heritage of the island. In Loíza, a town in northeastern Puerto Rico, Las Fiestas de Santiago Apóstol (the Feasts of Santiago Apostle) celebrates the battle between Christians and Moors in Spain. This is one of the Puerto Rican festivals that features the *vejigante*, a carnival character who blends African, Spanish, and Caribbean influences. Las Fiestas de Santiago Apóstol merges African gods and Catholic saints. In addition to his Christian roots, Santiago also represents Ogun, the African Yoruba god of war. And the vejigante is a symbol of the Moors' resistance to Catholicism.[16]

THE NEW BIG BUSINESS

Tourism is big business on Puerto Rico. In 1995, Puerto Rico reported more than four million visitors on the island, and it estimated that visitors spent more than $1.8 billion on hotels, restaurants, and recreation.

— THE TALES OF JUAN BOBO —

Juan Bobo stories are favorite folktales in Puerto Rico. They are stories of the "wise" fool who is honest and happy. They poke fun at the pompous "airs" that rich folk put on. A short example:

Juan Bobo's mother goes to church and tells Juan Bobo to stay home and watch the pig. His mother puts on one of her best dresses, carefully applies her makeup, and styles her hair. She feels truly gorgeous as she strolls off to church. The pig, though, seems sad. Juan Bobo tries to make him happy. He offers him food (pork!). He offers him water. Then he decides he knows what is the matter with the pig. It wants to go to church. Juan Bobo dresses up the pig as he has seen his mother dress up. He puts his mother's other best dress on the pig, then adds earrings, necklaces, and bracelets. Then he sends the pig off.

Of course, the pig finds the first mud hole it can and rolls in it. Meanwhile, Juan Bobo's mother comes happily home from church and discovers the pig in her best clothing. She is horrified on two counts: her best clothes are in the mud, and the pig is making a fool of her in public. As the story ends, Juan Bobo is in a lot of trouble.

Because of this story, people in Puerto Rico now know what to call individuals who dress up and put on airs. They call them *la puerca de Juan Bobo* (Juan Bobo's pig).[17]

The Puerto Rican tourist industry includes everything from huge luxury hotels to straw hats sold by kids on the beach.

The beaches are some of the biggest attractions to Puerto Rico's tourists. The island is ringed with *balnearios* (public beaches). These beaches attract people who need hotels to sleep in and restaurants to eat in and who want to buy a few souvenirs to take home with them, too.

Hotels provide jobs for managers, clerks, and cleaning crews. Restaurants provide jobs for managers, cooks, waiters, and cleanup crews. Golf courses employ people as greenskeepers, pros, shop helpers, and

— ATTRACTING THE TOURIST TRADE —

Puerto Rico tourist attractions bring revenue to the island in a variety of ways. For example:

- Near Utuado, guided tours and snacks are sold at a massive network of underground caves called the Rio Camuy Cave Park.
- In Ponce, the Parque de Bombas, one of the oldest volunteer firehouses on American soil, attracts thousands of visitors every year. They come to photograph its bright red-and-black-striped exterior. Nearby businesses sell souvenirs to these same tourists.
- The Tibes Indian Ceremonial Center, close to Ponce, draws visitors to see the remains of a Taíno village that dates back to A.D. 700.
- Coamo, the site of a thermal spring, attracts people who have heard the legend—the Taínos told Ponce de León that this spring was a fountain of youth.
- At La Paguera, boat owners sell trips to see the bioluminescent bay at night. There the water glows with millions of dinoflagellates that light up when disturbed by movement.
- The only tropical rain forest in the United States is located on El Yunque mountain. It attracts tourists to the Caribbean National Forest.
- The Arecibo Observatory in Puerto Rico, the largest radar/radio telescope in the world, attracts science-minded visitors. The observatory consists of a huge, bowl-shaped reflector 1,000 feet in diameter and a receiving structure suspended 650 feet above the reflector. Scientists there chart gas clouds, pulsars, quasars, and distant galaxies. Tourists get a glimpse of the universe.

restaurant and hotel crews. Museums and the tourist attractions that dot the island create jobs for museum crews and tour directors.

All of these businesses and parks attract tourist dollars, but the income goes not just into their own cash registers. The surrounding businesses benefit as well. Car rentals make money providing cars, and local artisans sell their arts and crafts to passing visitors. When employees at a large hotel or other tourist business are paid well, they buy food from the local grocery store, clothes from local retailers, and cars and gasoline for those cars. Tourism, then, becomes an interwoven part of the local economic network.

OTHER ISLAND BUSINESSES

Tourism has far outstripped what was once the island's most important business, farming. Only about 3 percent of the island's workforce is now employed in agriculture. In 1995, farming accounted for only $365 million of the $42.3 billion gross domestic product.[18]

Yet the island remains lush in its vegetation, and agriculture is intense in some regions. Sugarcane and pineapples grow abundantly along the coast, and sugarcane is still grown on some of the hillsides. In the mountains that range through the center of Puerto Rico, farmers grow coffee and bananas. Puerto Ricans also raise poultry and produce milk products.

Another business that has been part of Puerto Rico's economy for centuries is the production of rum, a distilled spirit. Puerto Rico began producing rum in the 1500s. The reputation of Puerto Rico rums grew over the years until today they are considered the best in the world, and rum production remains an important industry for the island. In 1995, Puerto Rico produced almost 26 million gallons of distilled spirits, most of it rum, and collected more than $50 million in excise taxes on the distilled spirits.

SAN JUAN–URBAN PUERTO RICO

The largest city on the island is the capital city of San Juan. This is the city that Spanish colonists founded in 1521, once they discovered that their first choice at Caparra was mosquito ridden. From that day until today, San Juan has been the premier city of Puerto Rico. The original sections of San Juan are the second-oldest European settlement in the New World.

Viejo (Old) San Juan is where La Fortaleza, the governor's mansion, was built in 1532. It still stands today, and the governor lives in it. El Morro, the military fort, which was begun in the 1540s to protect San Juan against invaders, is part of Viejo San Juan, too. These old buildings and reminders of the past stand shoulder to shoulder with today's version of modern Puerto Rico.

The city is cosmopolitan, complete with skyscrapers, posh nightclubs, wide boulevards, and crowded intersections. Along the Avenida Ashford, a section known as the Gold Coast, is a row of luxury hotels. And on the Avenida Ponce de Leon is El Capitolio, the Capitol, with its administrative and legislative offices.

San Juan Harbor is a busy seaport. The fourth-largest container port in the Western Hemisphere, it is the scene of great shipping activity. Seagoing vessels from barges to cruise ships sail in and out of the harbor every day. Across town, the Luis Muñoz Marín International Airport is another busy, modern transportation site. Every year more than nine million people fly in or out of the airport.

San Juan is the capital of Puerto Rico and home to about 438,000 Puerto Ricans. It has all the major problems of other modern cities, too.

CRIME AND DISEASE

Though San Juan suffers from these problems more than the rest of the island, Puerto Rico as a whole is fighting high rates of crime, drug trafficking, and AIDS (Acquired Immune Deficiency Syndrome). In fact, the crime rate in Puerto Rico reached such a high in 1993 that the National Guard was called up to patrol the beaches and shopping malls and restaurant districts.

The number of murders on the island nearly doubled in three years between 1989 and 1992, going from 467 to 862. The murder rate was 22.6 per 100,000 people in 1991. (On the U.S. mainland the murder rate that year was 9.8 per 100,000.) The number of robberies and assaults was also up. In 1992, the police reported sixty-eight robberies a day, up 20 percent from the year before. People in Puerto Rico were frightened. They built walls around their neighborhoods, put bars on their windows, hired security guards, and stopped going out to restaurants and nightclubs at night.

Why was there such a sudden rise in crime? Officials thought it was because of a rise in the use of crack cocaine, which began at about the same time as the rise in crime. "We calculate that most of the murders and robberies are related to drugs, and we know we cannot control the crime problem until we control the drug problem," said Governor Pedro J. Rosselló in 1993.[19]

Along with the crack, Puerto Rico also found it had a problem with heroin, marijuana, and cocaine. Drug dealers used Puerto Rico as a convenient entryway for drugs moving from Colombia into the United States. Colombian drug smugglers made Puerto Rico the center for their operations. They could drop the drugs into the ocean off Puerto Rico's shores and then send them to New York, Boston, and Miami in the suitcases of innocent-looking Americans.

At the same time, many of the drugs stayed in Puerto Rico, sold to the island residents. Puerto Rico has become one of the largest centers of heroin addiction in the United States, said one Drug Enforcement Administration official.[20]

Sadly, the drug problem goes even further—to AIDS. The rate of AIDS infection in Puerto Rico is the third highest in the nation, ranking after that of Washington, D.C., and New York State. AIDS is reaching deeply into the homes of Puerto Rico. Women are getting the disease at a higher rate in Puerto Rico than elsewhere.

Drug use has led to shared needles and the spread of the disease. Of the men who found they were infected in 1994, 57 percent got AIDS through drug use. Of the women who were newly infected, 53 percent got it from men, while 41 percent got it through drug use. Many of the women were married and thought they were safe, but for some of them, their husband's drug use brought the disease home to them and to their children.[21]

In 1995, Puerto Rican authorities took measures to reduce the island's crime problems. They increased the number of police on the streets to make neighborhoods safer. They stepped up raids and confiscated weapons, ammunition, and cars used in drug trafficking. Authorities also enacted stiffer prison sentences for drug offenders. These efforts seemed to work. By mid 1995, homicides had fallen 18 percent compared to the prior year.

Drugs are the dark side of today's Puerto Rico. Officials hope that drugs and the crime and AIDS that go with drugs will be a temporary crisis on the island.

MADE IN PUERTO RICO, U.S.A.

American business has been attracted to Puerto Rico for several reasons. One is that because Puerto Ricans are American citizens, the "made in U.S.A." label goes on its products. Also, tariff laws (the tax on importing goods into the United States) do not usually apply to Puerto Rico.

Another reason American businesses like Puerto Rico is because the island is close to the mainland. Goods sail to New York out of San Juan Harbor in as little as two and a half days. Also, because shipments to the mainland are going from one U.S. port to another U.S. port, no special international paperwork is necessary. These are qualities that businesses look for when deciding where to locate.

Labor is cheaper in Puerto Rico, too, and this has been a major reason for U.S. companies to locate there. The Puerto Rican Department of Labor and Human Resources reports that in 1993, Puerto Ricans working in petroleum refining averaged $5.23 less per hour than did mainland employees. In the manufacture of chemical products, employees averaged $4.22 less; those working in electronics averaged $4.12 less.

The most compelling reason for companies to come to Puerto Rico, though, has been the string of special tax rates that began as Operation Bootstrap in the 1940s. Section 936 of the U.S. Internal Revenue Code still provides tax credits for corporations that set up businesses in Puerto Rico.

Today, a few of the rules have changed. In 1993, President Clinton led a campaign to do away with the special tax breaks. He was not able to win that political battle, but he did reduce the tax credits. However, they remain large enough to attract business to the island.

For Puerto Rico, the result of the tax breaks have been good and bad. On the negative side, many complain that businesses have come to Puerto Rico, taken advantage of the tax breaks, and then quickly left before they had to pay any taxes to Puerto Rico. Also, when they left, their employees were out of work. And, with an unemployment level of almost 14 percent in 1995,[22] Puerto Rico needs jobs.

On the positive side, the tax breaks have "attracted billions of dollars of investment from U.S. industries," says one reporter. And they have created "an estimated 300,000 direct and indirect jobs on the island."[23] Some estimate that 11 percent of the island's jobs are with companies operating under Section 936.[24]

Industries have indeed established plants on Puerto Rico. Spread across the island in large towns and small are many well-known American companies. Pharmaceutical (drug) companies and electronics companies, especially, have found a home in Puerto Rico. The drug companies include (as of 1994) Eli Lilly and Company, Bristol-Myers Squibb Company, Johnson and Johnson, the Upjohn Company, and Amgen. In electronics, companies with business operations in Puerto Rico include Microsoft, Motorola, Inc., Westinghouse Electric Corp., and Intel Corp. Also there are plants for Procter and Gamble Company, Sara Lee Corp., the Coca-Cola Company, and the Clorox Company—and there are many more. Clearly, the tax breaks have attracted some of America's foremost businesses.

Puerto Rico is in an excellent position, say some of its leaders, to become a financial center for all of Latin America. The island has more than 350 commercial bank branches with combined total assets of more than $23 million. The tops of San Juan skyscrapers carry names such as Chase, Citibank, and Banco Popular. What's more, Puerto Rico has a bilingual population, which makes it a good bridge between the United States and Latin America. It has a stable, dollar-based economy. It is located near the mainland United States as well as near Latin American countries.[25] Said Governor Rosselló, "As bilingual and bicultural United

States citizens, we fully expect to assume a . . . responsibility for helping to bring the Americas together."[26]

UNITED STATES MILITARY IN PUERTO RICO

The people are the country. And in past years, especially during World War II, the people of Puerto Rico were very generous in lending their land to the U.S. military for bases there. But many of the bases remained after the end of the war, and some people became unhappy about that fact. Their "loans" of land became permanent possessions of the U.S. military.

Some of the acres have now been returned, but some have not. Over the years, nationalist Puerto Ricans, especially, have protested against the continued operation of the bases. Still, today, several acres in San Juan are devoted to the Navy and Army, and on the east coast of Puerto Rico, Roosevelt Roads is a large naval reserve. Of course, the bases do bring dollars to the surrounding communities. As in the tourist business, there is a ripple effect on the economy when a base is located in a town. Military bases employ civilians; military people go into the local community and spend money. Therefore, many Puerto Ricans want these bases to remain.

Puerto Ricans are somewhat united, though, in wanting one particular base closed. It is on the island of Vieques. The Isla de Vieques is a Puerto Rican stretch of land southeast of the main island. Most of the island was taken over by the Navy during World War II. When the base was built, thousands of islanders were moved off Vieques, and 65 percent of the island was taken over by the government.[27] Today, 50 percent of the island is still federal land and is often used for military and bombing practice maneuvers.

In 1995, the three Puerto Rican Americans serving in the United States Congress drafted a bill asking for the return of part of the island. U.S. Congressman Luis Gutiérrez submitted the bill to the House. With the end of the Cold War, argued Gutiérrez, the training exercises the military stages there were not only no longer necessary; they were *indefendibles* (inexcusable).[28] It was time to return the land to the Puerto Ricans.

The military bases, the large corporations, skyscrapers, and the big business of tourism blend together in Puerto Rico's current economic picture. Beside them stand the problems that Puerto Rico shares with other modern communities, such as drugs and crime. Alongside these stand the beauty and humanity of Puerto Rico, the traditional and the cosmopolitan. Truly this is an island of great contrasts.

Puerto Ricans in favor of staying a commonwealth
celebrate victory in the November 14, 1993, national
election. Almost three-quarters of Puerto Rico's registered
voters cast ballots to decide Puerto Rico's future.

FIVE

THE PASSIONS OF ISLAND POLITICS

Whatever [Puerto Ricans] decide, I will support.

—PRESIDENT CLINTON

When Puerto Rico became a part of the United States, it was seen simply as a war trophy. In fact, during the Spanish-American War of 1898, President William McKinley said: "While we are conducting war and until its conclusion, we must keep all we can get. When the war is over we must keep what we want." The United States wanted Puerto Rico.

Why would such a huge country as the United States want a poor, largely uneducated country the size of Connecticut? One reason became clear to United States politicians immediately. If Puerto Rico became independent, another country might be able to take it over. This would make the United States uncomfortable because, from the U.S. point of view, Puerto Rico sits in a strategic spot on the globe.

Puerto Rico is just 1,000 miles southeast of Miami, Florida, and, as the United States has proven over the years, it makes a good spot for military bases. As of 1994, the United States had twelve military installations in Puerto Rico,[1] and these bases served the United States well throughout the different wars of the twentieth century.

What's more, during the long years of the Cold War between the Soviet Union and the United States, Puerto Rico served the United States in an additional way. As the United States and the Soviet Union competed against each other to win influence over the world's countries, Cuba became a showcase for successful communism—an elegant showcase from the Soviet perspective, because Cuba sits even closer to the United States border than does Puerto Rico. Meanwhile, Puerto Rico became a showcase for American democracy. Former president Ronald Reagan said that " . . . to show the world that the American idea can work in Puerto Rico is to show that our idea can work everywhere."[2] Both the United States and the Soviet Union showered privileges and funds onto these two small islands in a hot competition to prove that its system was the best system.

The end of the Cold War, symbolized by the fall of the Berlin Wall in 1989, was a powerful change in world politics. It affected economies and governments everywhere in the world, including the Caribbean. Political analysts talked about finding a new pattern of thinking and a new way of looking at global relations. The United States, though satisfied with its relationship with Puerto Rico, did not need the island as a showcase anymore. Puerto Rico, meanwhile, asked itself if it needed the United States anymore.

THE GREAT STATUS DEBATE

Puerto Rico's relationship to the United States is a factor in all island politics. In fact, Puerto Rico's three major political parties are divided over precisely this question. The Popular Democratic Party favors continued commonwealth status; the New Progressive Party favors statehood; the Independence Party wants independence. Commonwealth and statehood place Puerto Rico inside the protective and supportive arms of the United States. Independence sets it off on its own, a friend but no longer automatically protected or supported.

The question of status seems to be a straightforward one, with just three choices, but behind the question lies the real story of Puerto Rico's politics. That story is about Puerto Rico's hundred-year relationship with the United States, and that relationship is the source of endless discussion and debate in Puerto Rican politics. A *New York Times* journalist recently called politics Puerto Rico's "most passionate pastime."[3] One of the most passionate questions discussed is: Should a nation of people—and Puerto Ricans are a nation of people in the sense of shared culture, history, and geography, even though they are not a separate, independent country—should this nation accept another nation having control over them?

The United States has final say over all federal welfare programs for Puerto Ricans. It also has some control over Puerto Rican business through tax laws such as Section 936. And since Puerto Ricans have no votes in the Capitol, many Puerto Ricans talk of going to Washington, D.C., "hat in hand" to beg for legislation and budget funds. Others simply complain of not being in complete control of their own destiny. As a commonwealth, Puerto Rico does not have as much clout in Washington, D.C., as a state does because when a state begs for budget funds, it has its votes as clout.

Puerto Ricans have held two plebiscites (national votes) to allow the people to vote on what they want their status to be. The first plebiscite was held in 1967. The results then were 0.6 percent for independence (most independence supporters boycotted the plebiscite), 39 percent for statehood, and 60 percent for staying with a commonwealth.[4]

The results, however, did not end debate over Puerto Rico's status. Years passed and debates continued. Then, in 1993, a second plebiscite was held. Emotions ran high during the debates for this plebiscite. "It's a tough choice," said Carlos Rivera, a Puerto Rican historian. "This vote goes beyond politics, and affects me, Puerto Rico, and future generations."[5] Puerto Ricans on the mainland as well as on the island went through a great deal of soul-searching as they argued the question. And the question, as it had been in 1967, was again: independence, statehood, or commonwealth.

The plebiscite is a chance for "the people of Puerto Rico to rule on their destiny," said Puerto Rico senate president Roberto Rexach Benítez, who favored statehood.

"It sets under way the whole process of decolonization," said

— BRIEF FACTS OF PUERTO RICO'S —
ASSOCIATION WITH THE U.S. GOVERNMENT

- Puerto Rico is a commonwealth.
- It has its own constitution to govern the island, but the United States provides Puerto Rico's defense, foreign policy, and trade arrangements.
- Puerto Ricans vote in presidential primaries but not in presidential elections.
- Puerto Ricans elect a resident commissioner to the United States Congress, but this commissioner has no vote. The commissioner can, however, vote in some committees in the U.S. House of Representatives.
- Puerto Ricans pay no federal income tax but do pay Puerto Rican taxes.

Puerto Rico senator Rubén Berríos, who favored independence.[6] Rubén thought of Puerto Rico as a "colony" of the United States, a term that implies that Puerto Rico is at the mercy of United States politicians. He hoped that enough Puerto Ricans would vote for independence to show the world that the United States held Puerto Rico against the will of the people.

Mainland Puerto Ricans couldn't vote in the plebiscite, but they held their own vote to express their opinion, and the commonwealth won. Whether or not they should express their opinion at all was hotly debated. Some felt that mainland and island Puerto Ricans are one community. Others disagreed. At any rate, it was a symbolic vote only. It did not affect the outcome in Puerto Rico.

Finally, on November 14, 1993, the official vote took place in Puerto Rico. Those Puerto Ricans registered to vote in Puerto Rico made their decisions, walked into the voting booths, and marked their ballots.

A majority of the Puerto Ricans made it to the polls that day. In fact, 73.6 percent of Puerto Rico's 2.3 million registered voters voted.[7] The results: 4.4 percent voted for independence; 46.2 percent voted for statehood; 48.4 percent voted for maintaining commonwealth status.

VOTE FOR INDEPENDENCE AND DIGNITY

When the United States took over Puerto Rico in 1898, there were many Puerto Ricans calling for independence. Cuba won its independence from Spain and the United States at that time. So the question had to be asked: Why not Puerto Rico? Over the years since, many Puerto Ricans have continued to argue for becoming a separate nation. Independence supporters have fought both peacefully and violently for their cause.

During the 1993 plebiscite, the Puerto Rican Independence Party (PIP) led the fight for votes for independence. Independence would guarantee "dignity and work," said PIP president Rubén Berríos Martínez. A country that allows itself to be governed by another cannot have dignity or true progress, he explained.[8] "Independence is the right of our people to govern themselves on their own land," added other PIP leaders.

So why didn't most Puerto Ricans vote for independence for their island? Possibly idealism would dictate a vote for independence. But the hard realities of life—getting food on the table and a roof over the head—usually rule a voter's choices. Independence for Puerto Rico would mean losing American citizenship and the ease of migration between the mainland and Puerto Rico. That could put a strain on Puerto Rico's economy. Also, United States welfare programs would be lost, and they are an important part of the economics of the island. What's more, American investments and businesses might go elsewhere if Puerto Rico became independent.

All these arguments are difficult for independence supporters to argue against. The island's economy is deeply interwoven with that of the mainland. But the PIP did argue and suggested that the United States could ease the transition to independence. For example, American tariffs on Puerto Rico's goods could be increased slowly, over a period of years. The United States could allow most migration to continue. In addition, the United States could budget a generous amount of federal money for the development of Puerto Rico's economy.[9] Independence, then, would not mean that Puerto Rico would be "cut off without a dime" the day it became independent. It would grow into independence gradually, and it would adjust to its new status slowly and carefully.

The plebiscite votes for independence seemed small, at just 4.4 percent, but some supporters saw them in a positive light. "We are the only party that has really grown," said Maria Cecelia Benitez. Another Puerto Rican independence supporter, Garcia-Passalacqua, interpreted the 1993 numbers favorably, too. He added the commonwealth and independence votes together. That equals a 53 percent majority of people voting against statehood, he said.[10] That meant that the majority of Puerto Rican voters wanted some form of independence from the United States.

VOTE FOR STATEHOOD AND DIGNITY

On the opposite side of the argument are Puerto Ricans seeking more, not fewer, ties with the United States; they seek statehood. "A star is missing!" writes one Humacao, Puerto Rico, resident. "The missing star is the star that represents a people blessed by God, kissed by the sun and caressed by the wind; a people who are humble and hardworking; a people who are a bridge between humans white, black, and red, a bridge between two worlds, the Latin world and the Anglo world."[11]

Add *estrella* (star) number fifty-one to the flag, say statehood supporters. And call it Puerto Rico's, because Puerto Rico has been a commonwealth long enough. It's time it became a state. It's time that Puerto Ricans left behind their "second-class citizenship" and gained all the rights of American citizens.

"Statehood is the only realistic option," former Puerto Rico governor Romero Barceló said.[12] Statehood would be "a non-colonial status with full political dignity," said the New Progressive Party.

Many Puerto Ricans at the time were confident that statehood would win. In the 1992 Puerto Rican elections, the people had chosen Pedro J. Roselló, leader of the New Progressive Party (PNP), as their governor. Roselló was educated at Notre Dame, Yale, and Harvard. He had won his election as governor in 1992 in a landslide, and he and his party support statehood. It looked as if the people had spoken: they liked Roselló; they liked statehood.

Statehood supporters made plans for after they had won. Winning the plebiscite was just the first step. Step two was getting people in the United States to want Puerto Rico to be a state. Already, former presidents Ronald Reagan, George Bush, and Gerald Ford had endorsed statehood. But most Americans had not even thought about it, let alone made a decision.

The plebiscite debate raged on. Economic arguments against statehood focused on a 1990 United States Congressional Budget Office study that reported that statehood would cost Puerto Rico 100,000 jobs by the year 2000. The island would lose 73 percent of its mainland investment. Its gross national product would drop by 3.3 percent, its unemployment rate rise from its then 16 percent to 30 percent. In short, the island would free-fall into a recession.[13]

But economic considerations were just one part of the argument against statehood. Cultural identity was a major concern of antistatehood Puerto Ricans. "If we become a state," explained José Santiago, a glassware worker in Vega Baja, "we'll no longer participate in international sporting events as Puerto Rico. We'll be representing the United States. I've got nothing against the United States. But I think losing our individual participation dilutes and takes away from our identity as a people."[14]

Statehood supporters argued back that Puerto Rico could have a *jíbaro* statehood. In other words, they could be a state and still hold on to their special heritage. Puerto Ricans could remain proud of their Taíno, African, and Spanish ancestors. They could sing their Puerto Rican hymns and salute the Puerto Rican flag, as well as sing the "Star-Spangled Banner" and salute the United States flag.

Dignity lay at the emotional center of Roselló's and the PNP's arguments—the dignity of becoming first-class U.S. citizens on an equal footing with their fellow Americans, of voting for the president, of having their own congressional representatives in Washington, D.C., and of bargaining with Congress as equals. If Puerto Rico became a state, it would elect two senators to the United States Senate and at least six representatives to the House of Representatives. It would gain a stronger voice in Washington, D.C., for its 3.7 million residents, and because its population exceeds that of twenty-six other states, it would be heard.

Another attractive point was that statehood would be a permanent solution to the Puerto Rican question. Though the United States admits new states, as it did in 1959 with Alaska and Hawaii, it has never allowed a state to change its mind and secede—once a state, always a state. The continual discussion and political arguments over Puerto Rico's status would be over, and politicians could focus on other issues.

When statehood lost by the narrow margin of 2.2 percent, Roselló accepted defeat. "The people spoke and I will obey," he said. But he added, "This is a struggle that will go on."[15]

VOTE FOR COMMONWEALTH AND DIGNITY

Puerto Rico should stay a commonwealth, argued Rosa Sánchez, a Hato Rey resident. "It has served us well," she explained. "We're Puerto Ricans with our own flag. If we are made to change, it will be irrevocable [could not be undone] and we will not be a people."[16]

The vote of 48.4 percent for a commonwealth was "a clear repudiation [rejection] of statehood," said Miguel Hernandez Agosto, the leader of the pro-commonwealth party, the Popular Democratic Party (PPD). Agosto and his party had fought hard to win the plebiscite. They, too, appealed to dignity as the emotional core of their argument—the dignity of maintaining Puerto Rico's Spanish heritage and the indignity of being melted into the melting pot of the United States as one of its states.

"We are Puerto Ricans first, second, and third, tied by blood and language to Latin America," said José Roberto Martínez, the PPD counsel in Washington. "We are not going to melt into the melting pot."[17]

The commonwealth status is "the best of both worlds," explained the leaders of the PPD. Puerto Rico gets the economic and strategic security of being part of the United States, while at the same time it maintains its own separate cultural identity. As a commonwealth, Puerto Rico benefits from the United States welfare and health care system, a safety net against recession and individual poverty. On an even bigger scale, the island benefits from federal tax breaks that attract large industries to Puerto Rico, bringing jobs and income with them.

Opponents to the commonwealth status point out, however, that the United States welfare system has created an economy of dependence. Instead of helping people get on their feet and encouraging them to build their own resources, the welfare system has encouraged people to avoid working at all. Possibly this system also fosters low self-esteem, they say. And they imply that welfare is partly responsible for the island's drug and crime problems. As for Section 936, that, too, comes under criticism. It encourages short-term, outside investors to open shop on the island, avoid taxes, and leave before they have to pay Puerto Rican taxes. What's more, opponents add, Puerto Ricans as commonwealth citizens do not share all the rights and privileges of U.S. citizens.

THE QUESTION CONTINUES

After 1993's plebiscite, José Roberto Martínez celebrated and asserted that the plebiscite results "put an end to this talk of statehood for a while."[18] Possibly he is right. Possibly the debate is on the back burner "for a while." But a victory for the commonwealth meant that the debate over status is not over.

Today's Puerto Rican commonwealth status is not a final solution to Puerto Rican desires and needs. The island's status is evolving and changing. Indeed, from the time the Americans arrived in 1898 to today, Puerto Rico's relationship with the United States has been developing, changing, adapting.

What's next in this relationship? Will there be another plebiscite, and will more Puerto Ricans then vote for independence? Or statehood? Can Puerto Rico be a commonwealth forever? Or is there a new kind of relationship—one that no one has thought of yet—that would combine the best of all three choices? As Puerto Ricans move forward in building their economy, these questions circle like seagulls over an ocean of answers.

Puerto Ricans who migrate to the mainland
strive to maintain their identity. Here they enjoy
a Puerto Rican Day parade in New York City.

SIX

MIGRATION TO THE MAINLAND

. . . a country that never was a melting pot.

—YOLANDA SÁNCHEZ

"I like los Estados Unidos, but it's sometimes a cold place to live—not because of the winter and the landlord not giving heat but because of the snow in the hearts of the people," Piri Thomas wrote in his book, *Down These Mean Streets*. He was expressing a common view. He wrote about the struggles of Puerto Ricans who moved to New York City to find opportunity. He wrote about the long, freezing days of outdoor labor during a New York winter and about the crowded family life in a small New York apartment.

Though his stories were fiction, many Puerto Ricans say he spoke the truth about life on the mainland for those Puerto Ricans moving to the Northeast from the warmth of their tropical island. The change from the tropical climate and close communities of Puerto Rico to the harsher climate of New York City and its independent people was a difficult one for many.

People don't leave their homelands easily or without feeling. The attachment to a homeland and a heritage is a deep human emotion.

Usually, there is a "push" out of the homeland by problems there. These pushes have ranged from wars to violence to oppression to poverty to simple lack of opportunity. Once pushed out of their country, people usually are "pulled" to another place. Something in this new place must be more promising than what's to be found at home or someplace else. Something must pull them toward the new land.

For Puerto Ricans, that pull was not immediately apparent when the United States took over the island in 1898. Even the granting of citizenship under the Jones Act of 1917 did not pull great masses of Puerto Ricans from their island to the northern states. Puerto Rican migration did not start to happen until it was "deliberately" started "by paid North American recruiters," say Alejandro Portes and Ramon Grosfoguel, two analysts who have studied Puerto Rican migration. They report that the first "sizable United States-bound flows [of migrants] occurred in World War I."[1] With the start of the war in Europe, migrant labor from there was cut off, and businesses on the mainland began to recruit labor from Puerto Rico.

THE GREAT PUERTO RICAN MIGRATION

A more constant flow of Puerto Rican migration did not really get started until World War II. During that war, more than 100,000 Puerto Ricans served in the United States armed forces. They fought in Europe and in the Far East. They also traveled to the U.S. mainland and saw the prosperity there. After the war, many decided to move north and become a part of that prosperity.

Their timing was good. This was a time of rapid growth of the North American economy. Once again, labor was needed stateside, and massive recruitment began. Mexicans were brought into the Western and Southwestern states under the bracero program to work in the fields there. Puerto Ricans were recruited by American manufacturers, especially those in the northeastern states, and most especially in New York, to work as unskilled labor. The Puerto Rican government, too, encouraged migration by providing information on job opportunities up north. Responding to all this enticement, men came north to work in factories;

women came to work in the garment industry, nursing homes, hotels, and restaurants.

During the 1950s, a period often referred to as the Great Puerto Rican Migration, the mainland Puerto Rican population grew by about 14.6 percent every year. In 1950, the Census Bureau reported 301,375 Puerto Ricans living on the mainland; in 1960, they counted 892,513.[3]

By 1960, close to two-thirds of all Puerto Ricans on the mainland were living in New York City.[4] East Harlem had become Spanish Harlem, and the South Bronx and Lower East Side (dubbed Loisaida) was rapidly "Hispanicized." In 1961, when Rita Moreno starred in *West Side Story*, a musical about Puerto Rican gangs in New York City, the Puerto Rican community there was well known and well established.

— A PUERTO RICAN MOVIE STAR —

Rosa Dolores Alverio (Rosita to family and friends) left the small town of Humacao in Puerto Rico in 1936 when she was five years old, and moved with her mother to New York City. The trip to the mainland from her rain forest home was an ordeal of twelve days aboard a ship struggling through storms. Once there, Rosita lived as most other Puerto Ricans who moved to New York City did at the time: in a tiny, airless apartment. Her mother worked long hours for low pay. Rosita herself sat in classrooms, but she didn't understand much of what was said. She spoke Spanish, not English. She learned English on her own, but she often felt stupid as she tried to understand what was said in school.

Outside of school, she learned to dance, to sing, and to act. Rosita's mother took her to auditions for plays and radio shows. When she was thirteen, Rosita acted in her first Broadway play. When she was nineteen she went to Hollywood, got into the movies, and changed her name to Rita Moreno. Today she is the winner of a Grammy, two Emmys, a Tony, and an Oscar— one of only three people who have earned all four of these honors.[2]

LIFE IN SPANISH HARLEM

In Spanish Harlem, bodegas (Spanish grocery stores) sold the ingredients for Puerto Rican foods. Here familiar fragrances from the island blended together to create a special Puerto Rican flavor—from *chicharrón* (pork crackling) to *casabe* (cassava bread), to espresso coffee. The bright colors of island vegetables covered bodega produce shelves—*chayotes* (a white or green squash), *amarillos* (yellow plantains), green plantains, yams, coconuts, green *quenepas* (a Caribbean fruit), orange pumpkins, and purple eggplants. At a bodega, too, cooks could find the traditional iron pots (*calderos*) used to make rice, or a *tostonera* (a special utensil used to smash plantains for *tostones*). The signs on storefronts blended American English with Puerto Rican Spanish, announcing *fondas* (family-style restaurants) that sold Coca-Cola and hot dogs alongside *sopas* (soups) and *arroz amarillo* (yellow rice).

The Nuyorican Poets Cafe, founded by Miguel Algarín, a famed Puerto Rican poet, became a watering hole for writers, musicians, and artists of all sorts. They gathered at The Cafe, and people from the community came to listen. Says Faythe Turner, an editor of Puerto Rican literature, "Many young people got their first encouragement at 'The Cafe,'" and The Cafe became important in the Puerto Rican community and in its New York history.

The place itself was not terribly impressive. "It was housed in what looked like an abandoned storefront church," says Turner. Inside were a few tables, a few rows of chairs, and an empty space for people to perform and for others to sit on the floor to listen. Beer, wine, and soda were sold out of a refrigerator to the side of the room. But in this sparsely decorated room, Latinos, mostly Puerto Ricans, shared their poetry, their prose, and their experiences of the world. The listeners, meanwhile, did not just sit passively; they "debated the truth or falsity of what they heard," says Turner. They examined the writers' words, turned them over, thought about them, and talked about them in their travels throughout the community. So the Nuyorican Poets' Cafe became a voice for the sounds and thoughts of the Puerto Rican community in New York.

Miguel Algarín himself has become a well-known poet, playwright, translator, teacher, director, and producer. Still, he is possibly best loved as the poet who inspired the Nuyorican Poets Cafe and as an activist for the Puerto Rican arts community in New York. He is a Puerto Rican-born poet, born in Santurce in 1941. He moved to Spanish Harlem in the 1950s and later earned a Ph.D. from Rutgers University.[5]

His voice is one of the voices that still reverberates with the Cafe's spirit. In one of his poems, titled "Christmas Eve: Nuyorican Café," from December 24, 1975, Algarín tries to explain the homesick feeling that many Puerto Ricans experience when they first move north. He refers to the familiar foods of Puerto Rican Christmas celebrations and to the warmth of the island's winters. In contrast, the Christmas season up north is cold and snowy.[6] This contrast between Puerto Ricans' memories of warm Christmases on their island and the cold holiday season they experience up north makes them long for Puerto Rico.

During the 1960s, the Puerto Rican population on the mainland continued to grow, increasing by about 10.8 percent every year.[7] The 1960s was a time of great reevaluation in the United States. It was a time of the civil rights movement and the women's rights movement. Puerto Ricans were thinking about their rights, too.

In 1969, a group of young people in New York founded the Young Lords Party. They staged dramatic protests on behalf of Puerto Ricans. In one, they occupied the First Spanish Methodist Church in New York City. It had been closed six days a week, and they opened it to the community. They also organized mass demonstrations demanding Puerto Rican independence.[8]

A MATURING PUERTO RICAN COMMUNITY

During this time, Miriam Colón, a Puerto Rican actress in New York, produced an important play. It was *The Oxcart* (*La Carreta*) by René Marqués, a famous Puerto Rican writer. Colón produced it because it is a masterpiece, but also because it is a story that is like the story of many Puerto Ricans who moved from the island to New York.

In *The Oxcart*, a family leaves their rural mountain home. First they move to the slums of San Juan and then to New York City. They are heading for the promised land up north. But the family never finds wealth or satisfaction after they leave their home. They find despair and humiliation. New York City is impersonal and the people are cold. They find that they have abandoned their home and their culture. In place of these, they have someone else's culture, and it is a false one for them. They are deeply unhappy. In the end, they return to their mountain home in Puerto Rico. They return to poverty and to hard work, but they return also to a life of dignity.[9]

The play captured the shock of many Puerto Ricans who left their own, familiar culture. The clash of that culture with the American culture was disorienting for many. Life in New York was different from life in Puerto Rico.

Miriam Colón wanted to show the experiences of the Puerto Rican community. She also wanted Puerto Ricans to be involved in the production. This was not a play put on by outsiders. This was a play by a Puerto Rican, produced by Puerto Ricans, for an audience of everyone. The play was successful, but more important, it was the beginning of the Puerto Rican Traveling Theater. Through the years this group has showcased over fifty plays by Latino dramatists.

The direction of the Puerto Rican Traveling Theater has been Colón's life's work. "I have created our own vehicle for the expression of our culture and our values without waiting for someone to create it for me," she says. She has passed on this gift of self-confidence to her theater participants and through them to the Puerto Rican community, and that has been one of her greatest gifts.

DOUBLE DISCRIMINATION FOR MANY

The world of New York was different from Puerto Rico in other ways, too. Many Puerto Ricans coming north faced true racial prejudice for the first time in their lives. Puerto Ricans come in all shades, explains Arnulfo Vargas, director of an adolescent program in New York City. "You can be Puerto Rican," he adds, "and look very different from other Puerto Ricans and still share the same values and heritage."[10]

Puerto Ricans coming to the mainland knew discrimination in

their lives on the island. But they had not experienced anything like the depths of the racial prejudice on the mainland. Here there is "a deep-seated conviction [belief] about one group being superior to another," explains Samuel Betances, a New York-born Puerto Rican.[11] Here there is racism.

A Puerto Rican author, Judith Ortiz Cofer, writes about her experiences with racism. Some of the prejudice was bold, like the boy in high school, whom she had a tremendous crush on, who finally asked her out. But his father would not let him date her: "Puerto Ricans live like rats," he said. Some racism was more subtle, like the time Cofer, then an adult, was stopped in a hotel hallway while on a business trip. A drunk Caucasian man sang "Evita" to her, a crowd gathered, and the man then sang an obscene song to her, featuring a woman named María. This insulting incident, Cofer writes, would not have happened to a non–Puerto Rican white woman. It was, she feels, not a terrible event, but it is an example of one of the many small insults that minorities face daily in this country.

Puerto Rican women face a triple discrimination—race, language, and gender. Yolanda Sánchez, executive director of the Puerto Rican Association for Community Affairs, says that Puerto Rican women want to change their public image. "What we're battling is the image of the Latina spitfire . . . hot-blooded, sexy," and very little else, she explains.

Sánchez points to today's Puerto Rican female leaders, to Olga Méndez, who has held twelve terms in the New York State Senate, to U.S. Congresswoman Nydia Velázquez, to Dr. Antonia Pantoja, and to Dr. Helen Rodríguez-Trias, a well-known public health activist. Sánchez gets frustrated, she says, because people don't think of these women when they think of Puerto Ricans.[12] They think of the sex symbol instead. Actress Rita Moreno was limited to the hot-blooded Latina roles for years. In fact, Hollywood dubbed her "Rita the Cheetah" in part because of the barefoot, spitfire roles she played. It took her years to change her image to that of the respected actress that she is today.[13]

The prejudice that all Puerto Ricans face when they arrive on the mainland is double—racial in addition to the prejudice of the English-speaking community against the Spanish-speaking community. This prejudice often causes an identity crisis for Puerto Ricans, a problem that seems to escalate for those Puerto Ricans born on the mainland.

"The single most crucial issue burning deep in the souls of many young, second-generation Puerto Ricans in the United States is that of the wider identity—the search for ethnicity," says Betances. From their African heritage, they might identify with African-Americans. But, says Betances, "Puerto Ricans who participate in all-black meetings find themselves apprehensive [anxious] when the anti-white rhetoric reminds them that the 'white devil' is just as much a part of [their] experience as [is the African] heritage."[14] Puerto Ricans embrace their own, unique racial and ethnic heritage, that of African, European, and Taíno. So more than ever, when they came to the mainland, they have to ask themselves, where do they fit?

IDENTITY AND ITS NAME

New words to describe Puerto Ricans living on the mainland, and especially in New York, have been coined over the years—names like Nuyorican, Rican, Neo-Rican, Nuevo Yorrican, and Boricua. One New Jersey Puerto Rican adds that he identifies himself as Boriken because the name keeps his Taíno, pre-European, roots in mind.

People searched for a new, identifying tag for themselves, especially first- and second-generation Puerto Ricans. Having been born and raised on the mainland, they were not just Puerto Rican but were also New Yorkers, New Jerseyites, and Chicagoans. They had a different view of their ancestral homeland. Many of them had never visited Puerto Rico. They knew of it through the stories their parents and grandparents told them. Many knew very little about the history of their homeland. They didn't study it in school and read very little about it in the newspapers.

This situation has not changed much today. Mainland-born Puerto Ricans often have a difficult time truly knowing their own culture. After all, they don't grow up in the midst of it. They don't absorb it in their everyday life. They grow up in the American culture, often in between the Puerto Rican culture of their parents and the American culture of their schools. Does this sound confusing?

It is confusing, according to Samuel Betances. In fact, confusion for young Puerto Ricans "may not be abnormal as all that," he says.[15]. It may just be very normal for all children between cultures to have to study those cultures and think things through for themselves. They have choices they need to make. They need only to study a little of both cultures so they can absorb what they think is the best of both.

One of the things that Yolanda Sánchez has done through PRACA (Puerto Rican Association for Community Affairs) is to help found Muevete (which means "to move forward with pride"). This is a youth program for girls and boys that sponsors a leadership conference to explore and strengthen cultural identity.

At the conference in 1994, Dr. Antonia Pantoja addressed another aspect of the question of what Puerto Ricans might call themselves. "Hispanic," a word that the media has used to refer to all people of Spanish-speaking heritage, was not an option. "We are not Hispanics, for there isn't any country named Hispania," Dr. Pantoja told the group. "We are Puerto Ricans; they are Mexicans, Cubans, and Ecuadorians, and you must not be lazy and clump us together, but learn each of our names."[16]

"It is being American to be a hyphenated American," adds Yolanda Sánchez. "This is a country that never was a melting pot. Eisenhower, a German-American, talked about it. Kennedy was an Irish-American. . . . To survive and do well in this society people have to have an identification which is not usually 'American,' but usually has to do with [the nation] where their original family roots were or religion, or race in the case of the African-Americans. People need that identification in order to strengthen themselves." And, she adds, "There's almost a glory in it. People romanticize the original homeland, have done that for generations."[17]

THE DREAM OF GOING HOME

Since the 1960s, the pattern of migration between Puerto Rico and the mainland has been one of ebb and flow. The Puerto Rican population on the mainland has continued to grow overall, though, increasing at a rate of about 4.4 percent during the 1960s, at 3.7 percent during the 1970s, and at 3.0 percent through the 1980s.[18]

Not everyone who moves to the mainland intends to stay. Some stay to work for a while on the mainland and then return to the island. Some stay a lifetime but dream of returning when they retire. In fact, in previous generations, a common dream of mainland Puerto Ricans was one in which they finally retired from work and returned to the tropical sunshine of their homeland for their golden years. Many actually achieved their dream.

The 1970s was a decade during which many Puerto Ricans returned to Puerto Rico. Juan Hernández-Cruz did a study in the 1980s that talked of "circular migration." Many workers came to the mainland, worked, went home to Puerto Rico, then came to the mainland again, worked again, went home, etc. A few studies that have been done since Hernández-Cruz's show that this is a pattern followed by some Puerto Rican migrants, but that the majority who come to the mainland stay on the mainland.[19]

CULTURAL GAPS, BIG AND SMALL

Life on the mainland is different from life on the island. Some of the changes are small, day-to-day changes. Tomás Ortiz, who lives in Texas, says his children made him change one of his island traditions. They made him promise not to rush up to them at their school events and plant hugs and kisses on them. In Puerto Rico, parents hug their children in public.

Frank Solano, a Puerto Rican who is the psychologist at the Puerto Rican Family Institute, talks about Puerto Rican affection, too. His mainland-raised children, he says, often seem rude when they're in Puerto Rico. He notices this when he takes his children to visit relatives in Puerto Rico. There, his relatives expect children to greet them with a kiss on the cheek. It's a sign of respect. Children who fail to greet their relatives with a respectful kiss are thought to be rude.

These are small differences, but they are clues to some of the bigger differences between the cultures, says Solano. And Puerto Rican youngsters who grow up on the mainland often wrestle with these differences, or with a "cultural gap" between themselves and their older relatives.[20]

Respect and dignity are values that are built into the culture. To uphold these values, children on the island are taught to follow very strict rules of respectful behavior. Meanwhile, children on the mainland are taught assertiveness and encouraged to express themselves fully. Clearly, children growing up on the mainland are going to feel some discomfort if they are being pulled between these two very different cultures.

The differences between the two cultures can seem overwhelming, and young people do need to create their own identity separate from that of their parents, says Frank Solano. But they also need to recognize the similarities between the two cultures—similarites in values and in human relations. As young Puerto Rican Americans take on responsibility, and as they accept the freedom that comes with adulthood, they are also exploring the two cultures that forged them.

Many Puerto Ricans have settled in New York City's El Barrio—a place of poverty and crime. But today, some are moving out of El Barrio to seek a better life in small towns such as Allentown, Pennsylvania.

SEVEN

LIFE ON THE MAINLAND TODAY

. . . to be somebody that everyone can be proud of.

—NYDIA VELÁZQUEZ

Today, New York is still the center of the Puerto Rican population on the mainland. Of the 2.3 million Puerto Ricans on the mainland, about 900,000 live in New York City and 1.1 million live in the state of New York overall. And New York City is not just the home of many Puerto Ricans today, it is also the site of more than half a century of Puerto Rican history.

One landmark that is closely tied to Puerto Rican heritage in New York is La Marqueta. In the 1950s and 1960s, this market, which stretches from 111th to 116th Street in Manhattan's El Barrio, was filled with Puerto Rican vendors selling foods and goods from home, fresh produce such as *yuca* (cassava), *ñame* (yam), *platanos* (plantains), or *yautía* (taro root), *pulpo* (octopus), or even a pair of *zapatos* (shoes) or a *camisa* (shirt).

La Marqueta fell into decay over the years, but it remains "the heart and history of El Barrio," says Yolanda Sánchez, executive director of the Puerto Rican Association for Community Affairs. She and her organiza-

— MAINLAND POPULATION: 2.3 MILLION —

The ten states where most Puerto Ricans live:

Percent		State
39.8	in	New York
11.7	in	New Jersey
9.1	in	Florida
5.5	in	Massachusetts
5.5	in	Pennsylvania
5.4	in	Connecticut
5.4	in	Illinois
4.6	in	California
1.7	in	Ohio
1.6	in	Texas

Education:

Percent

46.5—less than high school
24.2—high school graduates
19.8—some college
9.5—college graduates or more [1]

tion were working in 1995 to restore La Marqueta. The history of La Marqueta is a compelling reason to restore it, but the Puerto Rican community has other reasons as well. Restoring this traditional marketplace would breathe new life into the neighborhood around it, explained Sánchez.[2] It would also encourage new small businesses to open and provide desperately needed jobs.

LIFE IN TODAY'S BARRIOS

Life on the mainland for many Puerto Ricans continues to be difficult. As a group, Puerto Ricans have suffered some of the worst poverty of any group in the United States. As of 1990, 30.3 percent of Puerto Ricans living on the mainland had incomes below the poverty level. This is compared to 13.2 percent of Americans overall, and 24.4 percent of all Hispanic groups.[3]

New York City's Spanish Harlem, El Barrio, is one of the images many hold of life for Puerto Ricans on the mainland. Puerto Ricans living in this area, along with others from poor Caribbean countries and from Central America, still endure some of the worst urban standards of living in the nation. In this neighborhood, says one Puerto Rican, "you must watch yourself and everyone else, because you are in another world; you are . . . 'across the line.'"[4]

Once across that line, the streets are dangerous, with criminals hawking cocaine, methadone, heroin, and other illegal drugs on the corners in broad daylight. Drugs are the basis of a whole set of violent actions. The drug seller on the corner is linked with another drug dealer, who is linked with another and another, and soon a whole web of crime covers the neighborhood. At every intersection of that web each person is violently committed to protecting his "business," so violence grows alongside the sale of the drugs. What's more, the drug user, once heavily addicted, is sometimes willing to steal and even to kill to continue to buy the drug.

But that is not all of the bad news. Along with drug addiction comes AIDS, so that AIDS has become a familiar fact of life—and death—for people living in El Barrio. "Drugs and AIDS haunt every man, woman, and child who lives here," says a reporter who studied the neighborhood for *National Geographic* magazine.

The area also has one of the highest rates of welfare recipients, and one of the highest rates of school dropouts in the nation. What's more, nearly half of all the households (48 percent) are headed by females, and this, too, is one of the highest ratios in the United States. Many women are shouldering the full responsibility for their families, as they raise their children alone.

Reporter Van Dyk describes his impression of what this means in real-life terms: The role of the women in the barrio is to "keep the barrio glued together." he says. "I saw them [women] day after day," he says, "walking the kids to school in clean clothes they can be proud of, waiting for them in the afternoons, making sure they got past the dealers. Women often make the difference between a child who survives and one who dies early."[5] But the fact is that many women are often not able to provide a good living alone, so their children live alongside them in poverty. "It's clear that things here are tough," says Van Dyk. "Life is on the edge."

Yet even amid the despair of poverty and crime, many people in El Barrio try to live normal lives. And many succeed. One woman, who runs her own garment-sewing business, hires local residents to sew for her and pays them fairly. Another resident runs a barbershop. Another hires local young people to work in construction. Others sell flowers or fruit or own the small shops that line the streets. "People are struggling against great odds," says Sister Judy Garson, of the Little Sisters of the Assumption. ". . . But people *are* making it."[6] At the same time, many Puerto Ricans are making it in another way—by moving out of El Barrio. Poet Rosario Morales writes a poem about Puerto Ricans moving on, and she calls it "Getting Out Alive."[7] Many Puerto Ricans today are doing just that.

A NEW PICTURE OF PUERTO RICANS

A 1994 study by the National Puerto Rican Coalition revealed some surprising changes in the Puerto Rican population. Puerto Ricans as a whole, this study reveals, gained considerably in the 1980s. Between 1980 and 1990, the average household income per person rose by 29 percent. This was partly because of a decline in the number of people in the average Puerto Rican household, but also because of a real rise in income.

Possibly most surprising in the study, though, was the difference it revealed between two separate groups of Puerto Ricans: those who were born on the mainland and those who migrated to the mainland. Those born on the mainland showed a 32 percent increase in income. Those who migrated here showed only a 24 percent increase.

The study goes further and "shatters" stereotypes, say the report's editors. The stereotype is that Puerto Ricans all live in New York City, and that Puerto Ricans as a group are at the bottom of the economic ladder. Also, many think that "in contrast to other Hispanic groups, Puerto Ricans have failed to do well financially in the United States."

But Puerto Ricans are not all the same. Although in 1960 close to two-thirds of all Puerto Ricans on the mainland lived in New York City, by 1990 only one-third did. Between 1985 and 1990, 86,687 more Puerto Ricans left New York City than came to live there.[8]

Many are going to small towns in nearby areas. Allentown, Pennsylvania, an old Pennsylvania Dutch town, is one place that has attracted a good share of Puerto Rican newcomers. They come to Allentown for the same reasons as do others who move out of the city. They can afford the houses, and these homes are a great improvement over low-rent, crowded city apartment buildings. The streets feel safe. The schools are cleaner and better stocked with books and educational resources. Allentown offers the good life in middle America.

Today, about one-fifth of Allentown's population is Latino, chiefly Puerto Rican. They've bought houses in the older neighborhoods of Allentown—houses with yards and porches, and trees and lawns. They've become neighbors with the townspeople, many of whom trace their roots to the Pennsylvania Dutch.

However, the small town is not without its problems for the Puerto Ricans who have moved there. The personal styles of the Dutch and Puerto Rican people are studies in cultural contrast. The Dutch typically are stoic, do not like to show affection in public, and like to keep a distance between themselves and others when they are talking. Puerto Ricans, on the other hand, typically greet each other with the *abrazo*, the embrace, and stand closer together when talking. "Picture a Latino and an Anglo talking," says one educator in Allentown, "the Latino is moving forward, and the Dutchman is moving backward."[9] Conflicts and confrontations have been unavoidable.

Non-Latino Allentown residents have complained about groups of men gathering together to talk, drink beer, and play radios outdoors on porches and sidewalks. They see the groups as ominous and loitering, explains a *New York Times* reporter, but Latinos see this outdoor gathering as natural. It's a way for close friends and neighbors to get together and talk about their days.

Moving out of a neighborhood where everyone is Puerto Rican and into a town of diverse heritage, these people say, has its drawbacks. Prejudice is one of these. A Puerto Rican high school student reports that she has met discrimination in school hallways—a white student told her to go back to Puerto Rico. Many other Puerto Ricans and Latinos complain that *blanco* (white) store owners treat them like thieves. One six-year-old girl says she keeps her receipts when she buys candy so she can prove that she didn't steal it.

But moving has its positive side, too. It offers opportunities to partake in the all-American dream of a real home of one's own. And, says Noel Torres, an Allentown resident, after a while you get to know your neighbors. Some of them turn out to be okay; some not. "We got good neighbors, we got bad neighbors," he says. "Some neighbors, I don't think they like Spanish people. I try to say hello a few times; they just turn their head." And he makes friends with those who say hello back.[10]

MOVING OUT OF THE NORTHEAST

Today, many Puerto Ricans have left the Northeast region of the United States entirely. Large Puerto Rican populations have developed in Ohio, Illinois, Texas, and California. About 9.1 percent of the mainland Puerto Rican population resided in Florida in the first half of the 1990s.

One New York Puerto Rican who moved to central Florida explained her reasons; she said, "We wanted to raise our son in a different environment, out of the city, but we wanted to own our home, and New York was too expensive. . . . For a lot of people, it's a dream to be able to own your house. . . ."[11] She moved from one part of the mainland to another.

Many others, moving to the mainland from Puerto Rico, have simply chosen from the beginning to live in places other than the Northeast. Tomás Ortiz, a Puerto Rican who has been raising his family in Houston, Texas, for the last ten years, explains why he and his wife chose Texas over

New York when they decided to move to the mainland. "We were attracted by the slower pace, the lower crime rate, and the climate," he says, as well as the employment opportunities. He's still happy with their decision, and though he and his family visit Puerto Rico once a year, they are rooted in Texas now, says Ortiz.[12]

SUCCEEDING IN SCHOOL AND BUSINESS

Puerto Ricans who have chosen to live in different locations show differing levels of income. The area with the highest income for Puerto Rican residents is the Los Angeles–Long Beach area. The National Puerto Rican Coalition study, published in 1994, stated that for Puerto Ricans, the mean income per person was $12,032. In Florida, the mean income in the Tampa area was $9,267 and $8,903 in Miami. In New York City, the mean income for Puerto Ricans was $7,989. In Allentown, Pennsylvania, it was $6,193.[13]

Although locations do determine income to a certain extent, possibly more important is that they also attract people with differing skills and educational levels. Education has the most direct effect on income. "Puerto Ricans who had not completed a high school education suffered significant losses in earnings, employment, and income [between 1980 and 1990]," reports the National Puerto Rican Coalition. In today's computerized workplace, unskilled workers are in less demand, and what is in demand is an educated labor force.

Today more Puerto Ricans are completing high school than in previous years (in 1980, 57.7 percent of Puerto Ricans age twenty-five or older had not completed high school; in 1990, this number dropped to 46.5 percent)[14], and more are completing college, too. This change in the young Puerto Rican population bodes well for the future.

"Schooling tends to have the largest positive impact on earnings," says the National Puerto Rican Coalition. A major jump in income can be expected with a high school degree. And further education opens up doors to careers with not just more income, but also more personal reward.

GOALS OF BILINGUAL EDUCATION

School can be an exciting experience, and it can also be frightening. For a Spanish-speaking child in an English-speaking school, it often is simply confusing. To help these students, bilingual programs of different types have been set up across the United States. The goal of the programs is to help non-English-speaking children learn English. But the programs remain controversial.

In some of the programs, children leave their home classroom for a period of each day and study English as a second language. In other programs, classes are taught in English but teachers use first a simplified English with visual aids and gradually add more complex sentences. In still others, students are taught in the beginning in their first language with English as a second language classes. Then as their English skills grow, classes taught in English are added to their day until all classes are taught in English.

Many people believe that these programs are doing exactly what they should be doing—teaching English. But many others question if this goal is the best one or, indeed, the only goal for bilingual programs. Rosario Morales, an author and poet, puts into words some of the emotion of the argument against losing one's original language. She talks about "the joys of writing with *all* our words," and she means the words learned at home, from mothers and fathers and family members as they gather around the kitchen table.[16]

She might prefer a bilingual/bicultural program. In these programs, children are taught in both languages. Their lessons are alternated so that some days they learn in English, some days in Spanish. The goal of this kind of a program is fluency in two languages and bicultural sensitivity.

Bilingual education has helped the Puerto Rican children who speak Spanish, but more must be done, say representatives of the Puerto Rican community. And they have set up programs to get things done. The Puerto Rican Family Institute, for example, has a bicultural program for adolescents. The Puerto Rican Association for Community Affairs has an alternative high school program that seeks to empower disadvantaged students. These group projects have made a difference in many Puerto Ricans' lives.

Individuals have made a difference for Puerto Rican students, too. One of these is Dr. Antonia Pantoja, who organized the first ASPIRA clubs in New York in 1961. (ASPIRA is a group of Puerto Rican students who perform social-service work in the community).[17] Pantoja has worked for educational improvements and sought ways to empower students throughout her career. While she was a professor at Columbia's School of Social Work, she taught people how to organize to make changes in their community. She worked to reform the New York City public school system. And, finally, she was the force behind the establishment in 1973 of the Universidad Boricua (a Puerto Rican research center and bilingual university in New York City).

Less famous individuals have also devoted time to making a difference. At Passaic County Community College, in New Jersey, José Villalongo started a Spanish literary magazine, *Horizontes*, to create a forum for Spanish-language poetry and prose for the community. Some of the students write in Spanish only; some write in both Spanish and English.

VOTERS MAKING A DIFFERENCE

Bicultural education and opportunities to express cultural heritage are empowering, and one change that can come out of greater personal empowerment is greater political power. Individuals who make a difference vote, and many of them run for office as well.

For Puerto Ricans on both the mainland and the island, politics have centered around the status issue for generations. Once living on the mainland, Puerto Ricans have not automatically shifted their attention from their island status question to their new local politics. In addition, many of those born on the mainland, according to one study, may "have little desire" to vote and participate in the political system because, in their experience, it has not done much to help them.[18]

Most Puerto Ricans registered to vote are Democrats. In fact, in 1992, the Institute for Puerto Rican Policy estimated that 70 percent of the Puerto Rican electorate in the United States belonged to the Democratic Party. Less than 10 percent were in the Republican Party. The rest were declared Independents.

In New York City, Puerto Ricans make up about 80 percent of the Latino registered voters, but many choose not to vote in elections. More than 60 percent of New York City's eligible Puerto Rican voters are not registered voters.

How can a community get representation for itself if its voters don't make themselves heard at the voting booths? This is a question the Puerto Rican Commonwealth Office addressed with a 1988 voter registration drive. Called Atrévete en '88 (Dare to Vote in '88), it cost $1 million and was headed by Nydia Velázquez.

Within a year and a half, more than 118,000 new Puerto Rican voters were registered. So the program was a great success. Even so, in 1990, when voters in New York City's oldest Puerto Rican neighborhood were interviewed about the ongoing campaign for governor, the researchers reported that "most people didn't know there was a primary." They knew about the upcoming plebiscite in Puerto Rico and of problems in the community, but they did not link their lives to their choices in New York City's political campaigns.[19] Clearly, there is a gap here. Politicians have a job to do—to reach and represent Puerto Ricans.

Non-Puerto Rican politicians have noticed the power Puerto Rican voters could have. New York City politicians saw that the overall Hispanic vote was about 13 percent of the city's votes in the 1989 elections for mayor. In politics, 13 percent is impact. That's why, when the next election rolled around in 1993, all of the New York City candidates running for mayor showed up at the annual Puerto Rican Day parade. They wore *guayaberas* (tropical shirts), and they courted the Puerto Rican voters. Puerto Rican leaders were pleased. This was a good beginning.[20]

PUERTO RICAN ELECTED OFFICIALS

Today, several Puerto Rican politicians are working toward the common goal of empowering their fellow Puerto Ricans. Groups such as the National Puerto Rican Coalition and the Puerto Rican Legal Defense and Education Fund keep track of politics, keep people informed, and work on their behalf.

Puerto Ricans are also often being elected to local and regional positions. A 1992 survey of eleven states found 143 elected officials of Puerto Rican background. (The states surveyed were California, Connecticut, Florida, Illinois, Indiana, Massachusetts, Michigan, New Jersey, New York, Ohio, and Pennsylvania.) In 1993, Puerto Ricans, who were 12 percent of the population of New York City, occupied 16 percent of the seats in the City Council.[21] Puerto Ricans are serving in many capacities. Some are municipal judges, some state supreme court justices, some school board members, and some city councilpeople. Others serve in state legislatures.

On a national level, Puerto Ricans are gaining ground, too. The first Puerto Rican elected to a national office was Herman Badillo, who in 1974 was elected to the U.S. Congress. In the years since, other Puerto Ricans have served in the Congress as well.

In general, Puerto Rican elected officials report that they are concerned with the same issues as other politicians. They are concerned about education, housing, developing more businesses, health care, crime, and civil rights. In specifics, they each have their own stories to tell, as well as their own concerns for the voters in their districts.

U.S. Congressman Luis V. Gutiérrez (a Puerto Rican) from Illinois promised his voters he would be "a new kind of congressman." He has focused on issues that include housing for the poor and controls over salaries earned by congresspeople. Also, he has focused on reducing crime in the streets of his home area. To that end, in 1995 he sponsored gun laws. He sponsored one bill to ban semiautomatic assault weapons and another to ban "Saturday-night specials" (cheap, easily concealed weapons). "I believe that taking these dangerous weapons off of our streets is a key to reducing violent crime and saving the lives of our Nation's Citizens," he told his peers in the U.S. House of Representatives in 1995. He also supported the Brady Bill, a law that imposes a waiting period for gun buyers.

U.S. Congressman José Serrano was born in Mayagüez, Puerto Rico, and moved to New York as a child. In 1990, he began representing the South Bronx in the U.S. House of Representatives. Serrano served as the chairman of the Hispanic Caucus from 1992 to 1994. The Hispanic Caucus includes the politicians who represent large Hispanic populations in the United States. Sometimes they vote together to create a more powerful impact on the rest of the Congress. In addition to this key role, Serrano has also supported bilingual education and health programs for the people in his district.

In 1992, New Yorkers elected the first Puerto Rican woman to the U.S. House of Representatives. She was Nydia Velázquez. The area she represents is also largely poor and working class. She says that she was moved to run for office by a sense of injustice. The poor conditions of Puerto Rican neighborhoods in New York angered her. She recognized a need for political power, and for the political empowerment of Puerto Ricans.

As a member of Congress, she says, "I never take no for an answer," and so she gets things done. She was the lead sponsor of the Family Violence and Prevention Act. She has fought for bilingual education, as well as health care for the poor. And she has also helped bring new low-income housing to the people in her district. One of her greatest goals is to involve Puerto Ricans in their own political destiny. "We need to take responsibility in life and try to be somebody that everyone can be proud of," she says.

Several other Puerto Ricans have been "firsts" in their areas. Olga Méndez became the first Puerto Rican woman elected to office on the mainland. And New York State Senator Nellie Santiago was the first Puerto Rican to be elected from Brooklyn to the New York Senate.

Behind the scenes, organizations help to mobilize people and to build the community into a political force. They work for better housing and opportunities for Puerto Ricans. They lobby for funds to build better schools and health clinics. They set up counseling programs to help people get rid of violence in their homes and gangs in their streets. They work together to empower people.

Says Dr. Antonia Pantoja, "We have to develop a community of people who together will be supportive of one another."

No matter where they live, on the island or on the mainland,
Puerto Ricans value family and the dignity of everyday life.

EIGHT

CONCERNS FOR THE FUTURE

We, the people of Puerto Rico . . .

—Preamble to the Constitution of the
Commonwealth of Puerto Rico

Threads of history weave into the fabric of today's and future Puerto Ricans—a colorful interwoven tapestry that mixes the threads of ancient Taíno culture, and of Spanish, African, and American influences. Puerto Ricans demonstrate their deep connection to their heritage in their everyday life, holding to their values of dignity while expressing concern for the future of their culture.

In their celebrations as well, they connect past and future. Every year, colorful and exciting *vejigantes* dance at the head of Puerto Rican carnivals that celebrate the island's blend of African, Spanish, and Caribbean roots. In San Juan, the Puerto Rican love of life expresses itself in an annual backward walk into the sea. The Puerto Rican Spanish Catholic heritage shows up in somber parades and religious rites. Meanwhile, the Arecibo Observatory—the largest radar/radio telescope in the world—continues to scan the skies in an attempt to define the earth's place in the vast universe.

The past and future come together in other ways for Puerto Ricans, too. Puerto Rico is dotted with small farms and ancient villages, many of them poor, but the island also has sophisticated, modern regions. The cosmopolitan city of San Juan boasts international banking businesses and elegant restaurants and clubs. Luxury hotels line the beaches, and tourists fly into Puerto Rico's international airport and sail in on enormous cruise ships. Electronic and pharmaceutical corporations operate manufacturing sites in Puerto Rico, taking advantage of the island's abundant, inexpensive labor and its "made in U.S.A." label.

Today Puerto Ricans see themselves as a direct product of all of these different aspects of Puerto Rico, of both the old and the new, of the rich and the poor. They see themselves, too, as a unique kind of a people. They are a people with two separate homes. Some Puerto Ricans live on their island home and express pride in the extremes of their homeland, as does Aurora Levins Morales when she writes that in Puerto Rico "the coffee blooms between hurricanes."[1]

Some live on their mainland homeland and express pride in their achievements there. They seek new ways to identify themselves, using words such as *Nuyorican* and *Boricua*.

No matter where they live, though, and even as they look to the future, Puerto Ricans are united. They are Puerto Ricans, and they are also Americans. They ponder how their divided population will remain united as a culture in the upcoming decades.

A National Puerto Rican Coalition study shows that Puerto Ricans can no longer be stereotyped. Probably they never could be. Rita DiMartino, whose mother was Puerto Rican and father Spanish, uses herself as an example of Puerto Rican diversity. "A lot of people have perceptions of what [we are] supposed to be," she says. "I wasn't raised Catholic and I'm not a Democrat. I'm a lifelong Republican and I'm Protestant."[2] She is also a successful businesswoman.

The coalition's study shows that DiMartino is not alone. Today's mainland Puerto Ricans are living in cities and small towns all across the continent. Some are struggling at low-paying jobs, but some are living well and are very successful. Some, like Rosie Perez, Jimmy Smits, and Rita Moreno, have become Hollywood movie stars and celebrities. Many are doing well in businesses and professions. There is no stereotype that defines today's or tomorrow's Puerto Rican.

LANGUAGE AND VALUES

The question of how important bilingualism is for the future of Puerto Ricans is frequently pondered. Puerto Ricans share the English language with other U.S. citizens, but Spanish is the first language of the culture. Angelina Cabrera, a Puerto Rican executive, explains that she sees language as a big part of her heritage. "My parents never let me forget my language and my culture," she says. "I am bilingual and I think that's very important in today's world."[3] Language is one of the things that defines a people, so the question of bilingualism, along with bilingual education for children, is an important one for the future of Puerto Rican culture.

In addition to language, values define a people and determine the future. The Puerto Rican culture values family and the big and small dignities of everyday life. The fear of becoming "Americanized" and of losing their Puerto Rican values is a fear that many ponder when thinking of the future. The famed Puerto Rican leader Luis Marín Muñoz warned of the difficulty of holding on to traditional values as the island became modernized. When industries began to open plants on the island, he wondered, "Was Puerto Rico turning materialist, losing its traditional graciousness, abandoning its soul?"[4] He sought "serenity" along with economic success for Puerto Ricans.

"Serenity," he said, "may perhaps be defined as the habit of seeing your world whole, as the living society of [people] and forces and facts in which you as an individual conduct your life."[5] Muñoz Marín's ideas on serenity showed that he hoped the future would bring more than just bigger houses and newer automobiles for Puerto Ricans. He hoped Puerto Ricans could blend their Puerto Rican values with modern society's material goods. Puerto Ricans, then, would not lose the dignity of their

— SERENITY AND THE CONSTITUTION —

Luis Muñoz Marín was a leader in establishing commonwealth status for Puerto Rico. His beliefs and concerns are still current and can be found in *The Preamble to the Constitution of the Commonwealth of Puerto Rico* (1952):

We, the people of Puerto Rico, in order to organize ourselves politically on a fully democratic basis, to promote the general welfare, and to secure for ourselves and our posterity the complete enjoyment of human rights, placing our trust in Almighty God, do ordain and establish this Constitution for the commonwealth which, in the exercise of our natural rights, we now create within our union with the United States of America.

In so doing, we declare:

The democratic system is fundamental to the life of the Puerto Rican community;

We understand that the democratic system of government is one in which the will of the people is the source of public power, the political order is subordinate to the rights of man, and the free participation of the citizen in collective decisions is assured;

We consider as determining factors in our life our citizenship of the United States of America and our aspiration continually to enrich our democratic heritage in the individual and collective enjoyment of its rights and privileges; our loyalty to the principles of the Federal Constitution; the coexistence in Puerto Rico of the two great cultures of the American Hemisphere; our fervor for education; our faith in justice; our devotion to the courageous, industrious, and peaceful way of life; our fidelity to individual human values above and beyond social position, racial differences, and economic interests; and our hope for a better world based on these principles.[6]

culture. They would add comfort to their lives and bring their heritage with them into the future.

The questions Muñoz Marín raised with his thoughts on serenity are questions still asked today: Is it possible for Puerto Ricans to hold on to the best of their culture while adding the best of modern choices?

POLITICAL CHOICES

People make a country. People define themselves and their culture. They also create their government. The people of Puerto Rico have been debating their political status for a century—whether they should be a state, or an independent nation, or a commonwealth.

Puerto Rico's governor, Pedro Rosselló, was sorely disappointed in 1993, when statehood did not win the vote in Puerto Rico. His arguments for Puerto Rico to become a state were both sound and convincing, but the arguments for Puerto Rico to remain a commonwealth were also sound and convincing. And those who argued for independence had good reasons, too. This latest debate over Puerto Rico's status led some to believe that there is another, new way of thinking about Puerto Rico's status.

Antonio J. Colorado, Jr., a former commissioner for Puerto Rico, says maybe this three-pattern way of thinking is "passé" (out of date). "The newest thing is what's happening in Western Europe," he says. "Different cultures, without losing their identities, are getting closer together." He is talking about Europe's Common Market. The countries there have joined together for a common citizenship, common currency, and common defense. "It's happening," says Colorado. So maybe this could be the pattern for Puerto Rico's future, too.[7]

As Puerto Ricans shape their future, both on the island and on the mainland, they are building a new pattern for themselves. Their pattern will include a cultural nation of people who live in two separate geographical areas. It will include two languages. It will have a relationship with the United States—in one of the already-known ways or possibly in an entirely new way. It will be the creation of Puerto Ricans, the people. And it will be unique. The island of Puerto Rico is truly a tapestry that is still being woven.

TIMELINE OF
PUERTO RICAN HISTORY

c. 1000   Taíno people occupy the island of Borinquen (Puerto Rico).

1493   Christopher Columbus, on his second trip to the New world, sails to the island of Borinquen. He names it San Juan Bautista.

1511   Taíno people rebel against the Spanish conquerors. Ponce de León's troops overcome them, and execute thousands.

1518   First slave ships of African people arrive to replace Taíno slaves.

1539   El Morro (means "headlands"), the fortress at the tip of the San Juan Peninsula, is begun.

1595   Sir Francis Drake (of England) tries to conquer Puerto Rico; Puerto Ricans fight him off.

1625   Dutch take over San Juan and burn the city, including a famous library, before the Puerto Ricans can run them off.

1797 British attack Puerto Rico. Puerto Ricans join together to fight them off.

1849 *Libreta* laws passed. Poor Puerto Ricans are made to carry passbooks.

1868 El Grito de Lares (the Shout of Lares). Puerto Ricans take over the city of Lares and declare it independent.

1873 Slavery abolished in Puerto Rico.

1876 Libreta system abolished.

1897 Spain grants Puerto Rico local government control and full Spanish citizenship rights. Puerto Ricans choose their own governor, Luis Muñoz Rivera.

1898 General Nelson Miles (of the United States) lands at Guánica, Puerto Rico, during the Spanish-American War. Puerto Rico becomes a U.S. possession.

1899 Hurricane San Ciriaco hits Puerto Rico, leaving the island devastated.

1900 Foraker Act passes. United States declares Puerto Rico a territory.

1917 Jones Act grants Puerto Ricans U.S. citizenship.

1928 Hurricane San Felipe destroys Puerto Rican crops, businesses, and homes.

1937 Ponce Massacre. Puerto Rican revolutionaries, calling for independence, take over Ponce. Nineteen die in a battle with police.

1940s Operation Bootstrap begins. This is a pioneering program to attract jobs and businesses to Puerto Rico.

1946 Jesús T. Piñero is appointed governor of Puerto Rico. He is the first Puerto Rican to hold the office since 1898.

1947 Elective Governors Act. Law allows Puerto Ricans to elect their own governor.

1949   Luis Muñoz Marín becomes first Puerto Rican elected governor since the United States takeover.

1950   Public Law 600 sets stage for Puerto Rico to draft its own constitution.

1952   July 25. New Puerto Rican Constitution takes effect. Puerto Rico is a commonwealth of the United States.

1954   Four Puerto Rico nationalists open fire on the United States House of Representatives.

1967   Plebiscite held. Puerto Ricans vote to remain a commonwealth.

1969   Young Lords Party formed in New York City. The group stages demonstrations for Puerto Rican independence.

1970   Herman Badillo of New York becomes the first Puerto Rican elected to the U. S. Congress.

1989   Hurricane Hugo destroys towns on the east coast of Puerto Rico and causes widespread damage.

1992   Nydia Velázquez of New York becomes the first Puerto Rican woman elected to the U. S. Congress.

1993   Plebiscite held. Puerto Ricans vote to remain a commonwealth, but the vote is close; statehood almost wins.

1994   The National Puerto Rican Coalition publishes a study that reveals changes in the Puerto Rican mainland population.

SOURCE NOTES

ONE

1. Aurora Levins Morales and Rosario Morales, " Ending Poem," *Getting Home Alive* (Ithaca, N.Y.: Firebrand Books, 1986), 2.

2. Robert P. Walzer, "Rosselló Signs Plebiscite Bill into Law," *San Juan Star*, July 5, 1993, 3.

3. Yolanda Sánchez, personal interview, July 1995.

4. Edwin Rivera, personal interview, August 1995.

5. Robert P. Schoene, "Prime Time for Puerto Rico," *Hispanic Magazine*, August 1993, 1-5.

TWO

1. Edna Acosta-Belén, *The Puerto Rican Woman: Perspectives on Culture, History, and Society*, 2nd ed. (New York: Praeger, 1986), 2.

2. Susan Suntree, *Rita Moreno* (New York: Chelsea House Publishers, 1993).

3. Christopher Columbus, "The Green and Beautiful Land," in Emir Rodriguez Monegal, ed., *The Borzoi Anthology of Latin American Literature*, Volume I (New York: Knopf, 1977), 7.

4. Ibid., 9.

5. Himilce Novas, *Everything You Need to Know about Latino History* (New York: Penguin, 1994), 146.

6. Bartolomé de las Casas, "The Horrors of the Conquest," in Emir Rodríguez Monegal, ed., *The Borzoi Anthology of Latin American Literature*, Volume I, (New York: Knopf, 1977), 27.

7. de las Casas, "The Horrors of the Conquest," 25.

8. Novas, *Everything You Need to Know about Latino History*, 147.

9. Kathryn Robinson, ed., *Qué Pasa* (San Juan, Puerto Rico: Puerto Rico Tourism Company, 1995), 13-15.

10. Arturo Morales Carrión, Puerto Rico: *A Political and Cultural History* (New York: W. W. Norton & Company, Inc., 1983), 32-33.

11. Aida R. Caro Costas, "The Outpost of Empire," in Arturo Morales Carrión, *Puerto Rico: A Political and Cultural History*, 15-16.

12. Ibid., 20.

13. Luis González Vales, "Towards a Plantation Society (1860–1866)," in Arturo Morales Carrión, *Puerto Rico: A Political and Cultural History*, 81.

14. Arturo Santana, "Puerto Rico in a Revolutionary World," in Arturo Morales Carrión, *Puerto Rico: A Political and Cultural History*, 51.

15. Vales, "Towards a Plantation Society (1860-1866)," 81.

16. Santana, "Puerto Rico in a Revolutionary World," 54.

17. Robinson, ed., *Qué Pasa*, 15.

18. Vales, "Towards a Plantation Society (1860-1866)," 85.

19. N.A., *Puerto Rico: Showcase of Oppression* (Centro Social Juan XXIII, San Juan, Puerto Rico: n.d.), Book I:5.

20. Alfredo Lopez. *The Puerto Rican Papers: Notes on the Re-Emergence of a Nation* (Indianapolis/New York: Bobbs-Merrill Company, 1973), 176.

21. Maria Teresa Babín, "A Special Voice: The Cultural Expression." Epilogue in Arturo Morales Carrion, *Puerto Rico: A Political and Cultural History*, 327.

22. Lopez, *The Puerto Rican Papers: Notes on the Re-Emergence of a Nation*, 176.

23. Babín, "A Special Voice: The Cultural Expression," 329.

24. Ronald Fernandez, *The Disenchanted Island: Puerto Rico and the United States in the Twentieth Century* (New York: Praeger, 1992), 31.

THREE

1. Raymond Carr, *Puerto Rico: A Colonial Experiment* (New York: New York University Press, 1984), 28.

2. Marcos Ramírez Lavandero, ed., *Documents on the Constitutional Relationship of Puerto Rico and the United States*, 3rd ed. (Washington, D.C.: Puerto Rican Federal Affairs Administration, 1988), 50.

3. José de Diego, "No," in María Teresa Babín and Stan Steiner eds., *Borinquen: An Anthology of Puerto Rican Literature* (New York: Random House, 1974), 233.

4. Carrión, *Puerto Rico: A Political and Cultural History*, 142.

5. Carr, *Puerto Rico: A Colonial Experiment*, 33.

6. Carrión, *Puerto Rico: A Political and Cultural History*, 153.

7. Ibid., 137.

8. Edith Algren De Gutiérrez, *The Movement Against Teaching English in Schools of Puerto Rico* (Boston: University Press of America, 1987), 9.

9. Himilce Novas, *Everything You Need to Know about Latino History*, 163.

10. Carrión, *Puerto Rico: A Political and Cultural History*, 165.

11. Ibid.

12. Ibid., 223.

13. Lola Rodríguez de Tió, "The Song of Borinquen," in María Teresa Babín and Stan Steiner eds., *Borinquen: An Anthology of Puerto Rican Literature* (New York: Random House, 1974), 84.

14. Edna Acosta-Belén, *The Puerto Rican Woman: Perspectives on Culture, History, and Society*, 2nd ed. (New York: Praeger, 1986), 10.

15. Ronald Fernandez, *The Disenchanted Island: Puerto Rico and the United States in the Twentieth Century* (New York: Praeger, 1992), 100.

16. Ibid., 116.

17. Carrión, *Puerto Rico: A Political and Cultural History*, 272.

18. Luis Muñoz Marín, "A Good Civilization," 19 January 1960 address to the Legislative Assembly, San Juan, Puerto Rico, excerpted in María Teresa Babín and Stan Steiner eds., *Borinquen: An Anthology of Puerto Rican Literature* (New York: Random House, 1974), 226.

19. Carrión, *Puerto Rico: A Political and Cultural History*, 277.

20. Carr, *Puerto Rico: A Colonial Experiment*, 167.

21. Claire Smith, "Clemente's Widow Keeps His Dreams Alive," *New York Times*, November 23, 1994, B15.

FOUR

1. American Automobile Association, *Bermuda, the Bahamas, and Islands of the Caribbean* (Florida: American Automobile Association, 1995), 119.

2. Luis Palés Matos, "Neither This nor That," in Julio Marzán ed., *Inventing a Word: An Anthology of Twentieth-Century Puerto Rican Poetry* (New York: Columbia University Press, 1980), 21.

3. Juan Rodríguez Calderón, "To the Beautiful and Felicitous Island of San Juan de Puerto Rico," in María Teresa Babín and Stan Steiner, eds., *Borinquen: An Anthology of Puerto Rican Literature* (New York: Random House, 1974), 32.

4. Jeffrey Schmaltz, "Hurricane Left Grievous Wounds To Land and Spirit of Puerto Rico," *New York Times*, October 1, 1989, 1.

5. Frank Solano, personal interview, August 1995.

6. Edwin Rivera, personal interview, August 1995.

7. Samuel Betances, "Race and the Search for Identity," in María Teresa Babín and Stan Steiner, eds., *Borinquen: An Anthology of Puerto Rican Literature* (New York: Random House, 1974), 428.

8. Angela Jorge, "The Black Puerto Rican Woman in Contemporary American Society," in Edna Acosta-Belén, ed., *The Puerto Rican Woman: Perspectives on Culture, History, and Society*, 2nd ed. (New York: Praeger, 1986), 182.

9. Luis Palés Matos, "Neither This nor That," 21.

10. Rosario Morales, "Africa," in Aurora Levins Morales and

Rosario Morales, *Getting Home Alive* (Ithaca, New York: Firebrand Books, 1986), 55.

11. Diane Telgen and Jim Kamp eds., *Notable Hispanic Women* (Detroit, Mich.: Gale Research Inc., 1993), 156.

12. Fernandez, *The Disenchanted Island: Puerto Rico and the United States in the Twentieth Century*, 256.

13. Tom Verducci, "Puerto Rico's New Patron Saint," *Sports Illustrated*, April 5, 1993, 62.

14. Carlos R. Aristy, *Puerto Rico, U.S.A.: Center for Quality, Productivity, Profitability* (Puerto Rico: Government of Puerto Rico Economic Development Administration, 1993).

15. Evaristo Ribera Chevremont, "The Castillian Language," in María Teresa Babín and Stan Steiner, eds., *Borinquen: An Anthology of Puerto Rican Literature* (New York: Random House, 1974), 279.

16. Edwin Fontánez, *The Vejigante and the Folk Festivals of Puerto Rico*, (Edwin Fontanez, 1994).

17. Felix Pitre [retold folktale], *Juan Bobo and the Pig* (New York: Lodestar Books, 1993).

18. Gobierno de Puerto Rico, Oficina del Gobernador, Junta de Planificacion, *Statistics Appendix, Economic Report 1995*. n.p.

19. Larry Rohter, "As Crime Rises, Puerto Ricans Retreat," *New York Times*, January 13, 1993, A13.

20. Joseph B. Treaster, "Drug Agency Says It Seized Big Puerto Rican Trafficker," *New York Times*, June 5, 1993, 10.

21. Mireya Navarro, "Women in Puerto Rico Find Marriage Offers No Haven From AIDS," *New York Times*, January 20, 1995, A14.

22. Gobierno de Puerto Rico, Oficina del Gobernador, Junta de Planificacion. *Statistics Appendix, Economic Report 1995*, n.p.

23. Robert P. Schoene, "Prime Time for Puerto Rico, *Hispanic Magazine*, August 1993, 2.

24. Gail DeGeorge, "A Hurricane Heads for Puerto Rico," *Business Week*, June 14 1993, 54.

25. Rosemary Werrett, "Puerto Rico: The Spirit of Success," *Fortune* [advertisment supplement] December 14, 1992, 165.

26. Pedro Rosselló, "Open Letter to Business Executives," in *Puerto Rico, U.S.A.: Center for Quality, Productivity, Profitability* (Puerto Rico: Economic Development Administration, 1994).

27. Ronald Fernandez, *Cruising the Caribbean: U.S. Influence in the Twentieth Century* (Monroe, Maine: Common Courage Press, 1994), 229.

28. Luis V. Gutiérrez, *"Gutiérrez Co-Auspicia Proyecto de Ley con Comisionado Residente Robero Barceló, Velázquez y Serrano para Devolver Tierras a Vieques,"* press release, 4 August 1995.

FIVE

1. Juan M. Garcia-Passalacqua, "The Grand Dilemma: Viability and Sovereignty for Puerto Rico" in Anthony P. Maingot, *The Annals of the American Academy of Political and Social Science* (May 1994), 160.

2. Raymond Carr, *Puerto Rico: A Colonial Experiment* (New York: New York University Press, 1984), 316.

3. Cheryl Brownstein-Santiago, "Puerto Ricans Face a Road with Three Forks," *Los Angeles Times*, January 6, 1991, M-4.

4. Ibid., M-4.

5. Mike Clary, "Statehood Seen as an Even Bet to Win in Puerto Rico Sunday," *Los Angeles Times*, November 10, 1993, A-5.

6. Lorraine Blasor, "Legislature OKs Bill Setting Plebiscite," *San Juan Star*, 3 July 1993, 3.

7. Mike Clary, "Puerto Rico Voters Reject Statehood," A-1.

8. Jenifer McKim, "PIP presents plebiscite definition." *San Juan Star*, 20 July 1993, n.p.

9. Carr, *Puerto Rico: A Colonial Experiment*, 184.

10. Garcia-Passalacqua, "The Grand Dilemma: Viability and Sovereignty for Puerto Rico," 163.

11. Abraham Lausell, "A Star is Missing" [Readers Viewpoint], *San Juan Star*, 14 July 1993, 34.

12. Robert P. Walzer, "Rosselló Signs Plebiscite Bill into Law," *San Juan Star*, 5 July 1993, 3.

13. Novas, *Everything You Need to Know about Latino History*.

14. Gino Ponti, "Status vote sparks variety of opinions," *San Juan Star*, 4 July 1993, 2.

15. Clary, "Puerto Rico Voters Reject Statehood," A1.

16. Ponti, "Status Vote Sparks Variety of Opinions," 2.

17. Clary, "Statehood Seen as an Even Bet to Win in Puerto Rico Sunday," A-5.

18. Clary, "Puerto Rico Voters Reject Statehood," A1.

SIX

1. Alejandro Portes and Ramon Grosfoguel, "Caribbean Diasporas: Migration and Ethnic Communities," in Anthony P. Mainngot, "Trends in U.S.-Caribbean Relations," preface, *The Annals of the American Academy of Political and Social Science*, 533 (May 1994).

2. Susan Suntree, *Rita Moreno* (New York: Chelsea House Publishers, 1993).

3. Francisco L. Rivera-Batiz, Ph.D., and Carlos Santiago, Ph.D., *Puerto Ricans in the United States: A Changing Reality* (Washington, D.C.: National Puerto Rican Coalition: 1994), 11.

4. Ibid., 113.

5. Faythe Turner, ed., *Puerto Rican Writers at Home in the USA: An Anthology* (Seattle: Open Hand Publishing Inc., 1991), 6, 197.

6. Miguel Algarín, "Christmas Eve: Nuyorican Café," in Faythe Turner, ed., *Puerto Rican Writers at Home in the USA: An Anthology*, 19-20.

7. Rivera-Batiz and Santiago, *Puerto Ricans in the United States: A Changing Reality*, 11.

8. Lopez, *The Puerto Rican Papers: Notes on the Re-Emergence of a Nation*, 326.

9. Nicolás Kanellos, ed., *Biographical Dictionary of Hispanic Literature in the United States* (New York: Greenwood Press, 1989), 179.

10. Arnulfo Vargas, personal interview, July 1995.

11. Betances, "Race and the Search for Identity," in María Teresa Babín and Stan Steiner, eds., *Borinquen: An Anthology of Puerto Rican Literature*, 428.

12. Yolanda Sánchez, personal interview, July 1995.

13. Diane Telgen and Jim Kamp eds., *Notable Hispanic Women* (Detroit, Mich.: Gale Research Inc., 1993), 287.

14. Betances, "Race and the Search for Identity," 436.

15. Ibid., 437.

16. Gina Amaro, "Muevete Puerto Rican Youth Conference a Whopping Success," in *El Vocero* (New York: Puerto Rican Association for Community Affairs, 1994).

17. Yolanda Sánchez, personal interview, July 1995.

18. Rivera-Batiz and Santiago, *Puerto Ricans in the United States: A Changing Reality*, 11.

19. Ibid., 104.

20. Frank Solano, personal interview, August 1995.

SEVEN

1. Nydia Velázquez, 12th Congressional District Press Biography, 3.

2. Yolanda Sánchez, personal interview, July 1995.

3. Rivera-Batiz and Santiago, *Puerto Ricans in the United States: A Changing Reality*, 41.

4. Jere Van Dyk and Joseph Rodriguez, "Growing Up in East Harlem," *National Geographic* (May 1990), 55.

5. Ibid., 70.

6. Ibid., 70.

7. Turner, *Puerto Rican Writers at Home in the USA: An Anthology*, 32.

8. Rivera-Batiz and Santiago, *Puerto Ricans in the United States: A Changing Reality*, 2, 31, 114.

9. Laurence R. Stains, "The Latinization of Allentown, PA," *New York Times*, May 15, 1994, 57.

10. Ibid., 57.

11. Rivera-Batiz and Santiago, *Puerto Ricans in the United States: A Changing Reality*, 114.

12. Tomás Ortiz, personal interview, July 1995.

13. Rivera-Batiz and Santiago, *Puerto Ricans in the United States: A Changing Reality*, 35.

14. Ibid., 88.

15. Ibid., 85.

16. Aurora Levins Morales, and Rosario Morales, *Getting Home Alive* (Ithaca, New York: Firebrand Books, 1986), 146.

17. Annette Fuentes, "New York: Elusive Unity in La Gran Manzana," *Report on the Americas* (September 1992), 28.

18. Ibid., 31.

19. Ibid., 30.

20. Todd S. Purdum, "Politics Mixes with Salsa on Fifth Avenue," *New York Times*, June 14, 1993, B1.

21. National Puerto Rican Coalition, *Directory of Puerto Rican Elected Officials in the United States, 1993* (Washington, D.C.: National Puerto Rican Coalition, Inc., 1993), 3.

EIGHT

1. Aurora Levins Morales and Rosario Morales. "Coffee Bloom," *Getting Home Alive* (Ithaca, New York: Firebrand Books, 1986), 61.

2. Diane Telgen and Jim Kamp, eds., *Notable Hispanic Women*. (Detroit, Mich.: Gale Research Inc., 1993).

3. Telgen and Kamp, eds., *Notable Hispanic Women*, 67

4. Ralph Hancock. *Puerto Rico: A Success Story* (Princeton, N.J.: D. Van Nostrand Company, Inc., 1960), 112.

5. Ibid., 114.

6. Marcos Ramírez Lavandero, ed., *Documents on the Constitutional Relationship of Puerto Rico and the United States*, 3rd ed. (Washington, D.C.: Puerto Rican Federal Affairs Administration,1988), 195.

7. Robert P. Schoene, "Prime Time for Puerto Rico," *Hispanic Magazine*, August 1993, 4.

FURTHER READING

Harlan, Judith. *Bilingualism in the United States: Conflict and Controversy*. New York: Franklin Watts, 1991.

————. *Hispanic Voters: A Voice in American Politics*. New York: Franklin Watts, 1988.

Hauptly, Denis J. *Puerto Rico: An Unfinished Story*. New York: Atheneum, 1991.

Jacobs, Francine. *The Taínos: The People Who Welcomed Columbus*. New York: G. P. Putnam's Sons, 1992.

Mohr, Nicholasa. *Nilda*. New York: Harper & Row, 1973.

Suntree, Susan. *Rita Moreno*. New York: Chelsea House Publishers, 1993.

Tashlik, Phyllis, ed. *Hispanic, Female and Young: An Anthology*. Houston: Piñata Books, 1994.

INDEX

ABOUT THE AUTHOR

Judith Harlan has written a number of books for young people on topics such as bilingualism and Native Americans. Her book *Hispanic Voters: A Voice in American Politics* was recognized with a 1989 Carter G. Woodson Outstanding Merit Award from the National Council for the Social Studies.

A graduate of the University of Arizona, Ms. Harlan also earned a master's degree at San Francisco State University. She lives and works at the beach in Southern California.